Here's to Not Catching Our Hair on Fire

An absent-minded tale of life with Giftedness & Attention Deficit- Oh look! A chicken!

Stacey Turis

Visit our Web site at www.staceyturis.com

Printed in the United States of America

First Edition: January 2012

ISBN: 0983827508
ISBN 13: 9780983827504
Library of Congress Control Number: 2011916313
Bohemian Avenue Press, Plano, TX

For Dave, Willow and Nikko

Susan—
Be beautiful!
Be yourself.
XO, Stacy
Turis

Introduction

Sitting in my bed, propped up by more pillows than necessary, I have my beloved iPhone next to me, running a Brain Wave application set to *focus*. As I adjust my legs crosswise and turn on my laptop, I close my eyes and allow the white noise and binaural beats to flow through the headphones and permeate every mottled-grey fold of my unreliable brain. I sit with the laptop balanced on my thighs for a couple minutes to allow for the full effect from the software. Though I would appear peaceful to someone walking past, inside my mind I have just stepped into a more chaotic yet colorful world. There are many layers, multiple dimensions, and an almost metaphysical knowing inside this brain of mine. With a seasoned hunter's keen perception, I'm aware of the soft sigh of the tea bag settling in the cup of extra-hot water next to the bed. My eyes move upward under my lids as my mind registers the constant breath of the ceiling fan and the distracting pinging noise as the pull-cord clinks against the base with every rotation from the blades above. "I'll need to turn that off," I think.

My toes spread out for a spontaneous massage of our cat, Yin Yang, who just so happened to claim the area next to my foot when I finally got situated on the bed. (I say *just so happened to* sarcastically, as Yin Yang is *always* waiting to lie by someone, and I'm pretty sure he has learned to materialize at will.) I feel his fur moving under my feet and smile at the vibrations that suddenly start deep under my toes. My nose wrinkles as I pick up on the faint fishy smell that emanates from Yin Yang's mouth. There are times, when my coping skills aren't at their best, that I get so bothered by the smell and sound of Yin Yang smacking his kitty lips, I literally gag (imagine a toothless, old person eating a banana). With that unpleasant thought, I realize that I'm losing my focus. I shake my head to clear the visuals, take another deep breath, and try to bring my attention back to the present.

With my eyes closed, legs crossed, and pointer finger and thumb touching in *Chin Mudra*, I take some deep breaths and throw out a request to the universe. *Begging* would probably be more accurate, but you get the idea: "Please, please, please bless me with a shit-load of focus, patience, creativity, and raw strength." I say *shit-load* to eliminate any possible confusion of how much of the above I really need, and I'm pretty sure God understands my reasoning and isn't offended by my colorful language. While my Vetiver and Cedarwood essential oils burn in a jar on top of the armoire, I use my entire arsenal to establish focus and concentration. I have to. Though most of my days consist of what feels like stumbling through a dark foggy swamp with an eye patch diminishing any possible visibility, this day needs to be different. I need all the help I can get. I am opening my laptop to begin writing my first book.

As my eyes open and focus on the screen, they reflect first shock and then recognition. They slowly follow the huge crack that blazes through the middle of the screen and runs diagonally from top left to bottom right. I realize with a grimace that this may slightly affect my ability to concentrate, as I can't see a bloody word I'm typing! I stepped on my laptop more than two years ago and still haven't replaced the cracked screen. I know it might sound like I'm a little lazy, but I'm not. Well, I mean I am, but I work on it all the time; it's always part of my self-improvement plan. Anyway my point is that laziness is not the factor in my still staring at this crack; it's because as soon as I power it down and flip the laptop closed, the crack leaves my mind, never to return until I open the laptop once again. Then I groan because of the big-ass crack that has once again surprised me with its presence.

I guess at this point I should introduce myself. Hello. My name is Stacey, and I am "twice exceptional." Sounds fabulous, doesn't it? I mean, not only am I exceptional, I'm *twice* exceptional! Don't hurt yourself congratulating me.

What it really means is that I have Attention Deficit Hyperactivity Disorder (AD[H]D), and I'm also considered "gifted." It's called twice exceptional because half of my brain is capable of astonishing mental feats, while the other half can't even bother to lift its leg when it farts, which isn't very productive, if you ask me. Yeah…try using that to navigate through life. It's a mess. A person can be twice exceptional in different areas, but I was blessed with the above. And no, I don't play a musical instrument, I don't sing like a canary, nor do I ever stop midsentence and begin writing math equations on the nearest window. As a matter of fact, there is not one certain thing I can claim to be gifted in. I'm the proverbial Jack of all trades, master of none. All of the guts and none of the glory. None of the sugar and all of the shit. You catch my drift.

Normally when I'm meeting someone new, I immediately become self-deprecating to make them like me. "Nice to meet you…great party. Yes, my belly is hanging over my pants to my knees from eating so much. I hope my breath doesn't kill you from the garlic dip. Is this crowd freaking you out at all? I'm sorry, what was your name again?" I know it sounds like I need therapy (and I do), but I kind of like that about myself. It makes people instantly comfortable, like they can scratch their armpits or pick the underwear out of their butts in front of me, and contrary to popular logic, that's a good thing! Anyway, I'm pretty sure all of the above was enough to disarm you.

I'm thirty-seven years old. I have a husband, two kids, a dog, three cats, and about seventy-eight fish that hatched from our original two. I never meant to have a fish farm, but then again, I never mean for any of the stuff that happens to me to, well…happen to me. I started my own holistic pet health site, founded a holistic charity for sheltered animals (I've received three donations: the entire start-up cost from my father-in-law, one from my mom, and a five-hundred-dollar check that I lost), I have a holistic health blog for families, and I recently put together a program to educate families about the benefits of clean and natural living. I am my daughter's homeroom mom, and last year I was on the PTA board, where I was in charge of the yearbook. (I'm actually still too traumatized to talk about *that* experience.) I keep all chemicals out of our house and feed my family only all-natural and organic foods. I buy only natural body products and detergents, and make my cleaning supplies with vinegar, baking soda and essential oils...you get the idea. As I read over what I just wrote, it makes me chuckle. It's all true, but I still feel like a fraud, because if any of that makes me sound like I have my shit together, don't let me fool you—I'm a fucking mess.

We live in a middle-class neighborhood. My husband, Dave, drives a ten-year-old bucket, which allows me to cart the kids and animals around in a big SUV, like every other mom in the carpool lane at my kids' school. Oh, except for Trinity Jackson...she drives a big, white Hummer with a vanity plate that screams, "TRINSH2." Don't get me wrong. I like Trinity. I pretty much like most people I meet, and I try not to hold their vanity plates against them. All in all, we have a nice, ~~normal~~ little family, and we enjoy living in the 'burbs, except for one tiny problem. As you can see by my double strikethrough above, when it comes to my life, *normal* is rarely in the equation.

Though I was coined *gifted* as a kid, I wasn't diagnosed with AD(H)D until I was thirty-three (after first being misdiagnosed with, and medicated for, bipolar disorder. Fun times). As giftedness can also easily be misdiagnosed as AD(H)D, I ran into the gifted concept a lot after researching my diagnosis. I hadn't thought about my gifted side since I was a kid. You can imagine how shocked I was to learn that both gifts have a tendency to create chaos in adulthood. It doesn't stop when you hit puberty, buddy. These are the gifts that keep on giving. I couldn't believe it. There I was, in black and white. My entire being of weirdness, easily explained with bullet points listed under both "Signs of Adult AD(H)D" and "Signs of Adult Giftedness." Double trouble. Twice fucked, as I like to say. Getting diagnosed was definitely a mixed blessing for me. On one hand there was a nicely packaged reason for all of the things I felt were wrong with me. On the other hand, it was comparable to a mental-health death sentence. I used to say to my mom, "It shouldn't be this hard...it isn't this hard for other people...this isn't normal." I used to think I could just fix myself away with my little self-improvement plans. I still do, actually—a different one every week, but getting that diagnosis meant I could do all of the self-improvement plans available in the universe, and I would still come out as messed up as I went in. No improvements for me. Sorry, Charlie. Shit out of luck, my friend.

I've always felt misunderstood. Though I was never at a loss for friends, I was always told I was weird, which I was totally OK with. *Weird* is a compliment, I think. I just didn't really understand what people thought was weird about me. It could have something to do with the following, but I'll let you be the judge of that. Thanks to my two gifts, I have a tendency to be anxious and depressed. I'm completely overtaken by the moods of others. I procrastinate. I can't pay bills or keep track of finances, and I have no emotional ties to money. I don't put effort into relationships, except for those with people who have grown to accept me and don't try to change me. I don't bond easily with most people. I constantly stress myself out trying to help everyone except myself. I feel a connection with nature in my bones, but almost to the point of pain. I get in a funk where I feel dead inside. I'm easily overwhelmed. I don't like to be touched. The sound of a telephone makes me want to put my fist through a wall. I have a horrendous temper and can snap but then forget about it five seconds later. I have horrible word recall. I often forget what I'm talking about midsentence and have to ask the dreaded, "Uh...what were we talking about?" I don't pay attention to getting to my destination when I drive and have ended up in the wrong state more than once. I love animals so much it can be painful, and I have the chips in my teeth from grinding them to prove it. I'm emotionally and physically affected by the sadness and heartbreak of others. I can barely sit still to watch TV, except for *It's Always Sunny in Philadelphia* or my favorite paranormal show, *Destination Truth*. (Call me, Josh Gates. Your show is my new dream job!) Unfortunately, I never remember what day or time they're on, so, thank you, DVR! Overhead lights bother me. A ceiling fan on my skin makes me crazy. Strong odors can make me throw up. I can't make casual conversation on the phone; there has to be a purpose, such as scheduling. "What time do ya want to meet? Two o'clock? OK, bye." I sometimes don't understand people if they speak too fast, and then I have to read their lips, which can be awkward for everyone involved. I can't maintain eye contact during a conversation, and if I try to, I feel like my eyes are going to pop out of my head. According to my hubby, I "have no regard for safety." There's more…a lot more, actually, but I think I'll let you discover some for yourself. A girl has to stay somewhat mysterious, you know!

Section One:
100 Percent Unnaturally, Natural Me

"A true man never frets about his place in the world, but just slides into it by the gravitation of his nature, and swings there as easily as a star."

—Edwin Hubbell Chapin

Chapter 1

I'd much rather go through a lifetime of my own torturous angst than to put those that I love through the pain of my self-inflicted "going out with a fart" instead of a bang to the head.

It's funny (as in *weird*, not *ha ha*) that most people's impression of AD(H)D is a spazzy kid at school that won't shut his mouth, wiggles in his seat, tips his chair back on two legs, falls on the floor, and then gets sent to the office for being disruptive. That's not a true depiction of AD(H) D! Well, actually, it is. We can definitely do all of that, but there is so much more to us than that. Some of us AD(H)Ders are not hyper at all—just a little (or a lot) inattentive. Though currently the condition is all dumped under a generic AD(H) D label, I still consider myself ADD since I'm not hyper. There are so many more layers to us than most would ever imagine. We are privy to a billion gifts and a gazillion heartaches. AD(H)D has the ability to ruin not only the lives of those who have it, but those around them as well. Families, marriages, jobs, relationships...they all display the scars from the battle that is AD(H)D. Nothing comes out unscathed—absolutely nothing. The remnants of unnecessary guilt and shame are littered about like debris on a beach after a storm. If we want to walk down the beach, we just have to step around it.

Some have called me *scattered* or *unorganized*, to the same tune they would call someone an *absentee mother* or *trash eater*. Those stupid assholes have no idea how destructive and ignorant they are with their words. I make myself sick constantly trying to be organized, trying to be "with it," trying to be a less-intense version of myself, and basically putting so much energy into trying to be a person that I cannot be—no way, no how—that it slowly kills me. I'll admit, though, that I can be a dumbass. It actually took me three years to figure out which garage was mine. In our city, garages are considered unsightly, so they build them off the back of the house with access from an alley. Three years! I do forget a lot, but it's not really the forgetting that gets me down. My personal struggle has always been the anxiety, depression, and all-around fogginess that seem to go hand in hand with this wacky brain of mine. Second by second, I'm trying to push through a barrier that stands between me and what I need to accomplish that day. Do you know the internal struggle I go through just trying to make myself go to the grocery store? Or to answer e-mails? Or to make the kids' lunches for school? Those little things that most would find slightly annoying, I find unbearable, which makes my life hell on most days. If that isn't enough, there are intense and painful feelings of self-shame, of being such a loser that I can't understand how anyone could possibly stand to be around me. Most of the time, I don't even want to be around myself! Can someone please teach me how to have an out-of-body experience? Anyone? My self-talk is embarrassing; I would never speak to anyone the way I speak to myself.

Unfortunately and fortunately, giftedness booked the same brain in the same life, and I'm stuck with both. Sometimes I have a problem differentiating which side I need to pull a coping skill from, but now, for the most part, I can sort it out. Whereas AD(H)D is contained mostly in the mental arena (I say *mostly* because sensory issues are also common), my giftedness has both mental and physical aspects to it. OK, get ready…here comes a freak flag! I'm an empath—at least that's what I've been told. I "feel" things mentally to understand them. It is kind of like a grocery scanner. I mentally hold a thought, idea, or person in front of my stomach and scan it. You can't imagine the amount of information I receive by doing that. It's not like it pours slowly in, though. It's more of an immediate knowing of many things all at once…*bam!* Information stored for later review. Scanning is just one way I get information and the only one I have total control over. But for the most part, I pick up information I don't want when I don't want it. Don't assume that I know a person's dirty secrets or what they had for breakfast. It's mostly feelings. Someone's negative mood or emotion can hit me in the stomach and just dig and dig and dig until it's raw and achy, and I have to leave their presence. Even then, the feelings don't go away completely. They always linger until I stop what I'm doing and focus on getting rid of them. Most of the time, I can't be bothered to try to stop what I'm doing, so I just deal with the underlying anxiety it causes me that day.

When I'm not at 100 percent mentally or emotionally and unable to block things out, I also pick up on feelings that aren't directed toward me, but to another person, thought, or idea, which sucks because I can't distinguish between any of them. I'm like a radar gun picking up every wave in my range. Beep. Beep. Beep. As you can imagine, I basically walk in a world of constantly thinking, "What's wrong with so-and-so? Did I do something to blah, blah, blah?"

On top of all that, because of the physiology of my brain, I get blasted from every direction. That's what it feels like, too—a continuous attack, not only mentally but physically. Smells, sounds, every sense is on fire every second of every waking day. It makes me feel like I'm in a never-ending state of trying to find balance on the edge of a slippery cliff. "Please, God, just let me make it through today. I'll worry about tomorrow if I get there." Toss in the constant juggling of everyday life, and I have to be pretty steady and on top of my game to keep my balance, which is obviously sometimes more than I can handle. Quite often, I panic, drop the balls, and fall. Anything seemingly minor can knock me right off the edge, but I struggle mightily to keep my balance because if I fall, I'll land in the *dead* place, and that place is no bueno.

This is how I once described a visit to the dead place, otherwise known as depression.

> The dead place is dark, lonely, and suffocating. The voice from the dead place talks to me and tells me that I'll never leave, that I'll be there forever or until I can't take it anymore and decide to "check out." I begin to believe it, because it's the only voice I hear, other than the faint cry from the other voices. The other voices are so far away. They are standing at the edge of the cliff, looking down at me and calling out for me. I can't hear what they're saying. I know they're trying to tell me something, but the voice from the dead place speaks louder. I get frustrated and confused from the noise, straining painfully to hear the words of the other voices, hoping for a way out.
>
> After some time, the other voices give up, turning away in frustration. I have no idea they were offering their hands and even brought a rope to help me climb out. Since I'm not holding my hand out in return, they think I'm simply ignoring them. They don't know that I can't hear them and that their voices are mixed and jumbled. They have decided that I must like it in that deep, dark, dead place, or else I would have reached for their hands.
>
> My stomach flips as the dark, heavy fabric of their frustration shrouds my head, making it almost impossible to breathe, see, or hear. The fabric starts to move and slowly begins snaking in and out of my eyes, ears, nose, and mouth, before settling heavily in my brain. Immediately my senses begin to fade, and my vision is replaced with the mottled grey-brown color of the fabric. My stomach jerks as I gag from the sickly sweet smell of it. Pain makes me recoil from the accusing heat of it burning my skin. I gag again as my mouth fills with the sharp, metallic taste of it. Confused, angry, embarrassed, and hurt, I begin to mentally disconnect and disengage from the other voices and their judgments. Doing so will prevent this pain in the future. Afraid of suffocating as the feeling of shame

becomes unbearable, I slowly turn away from those in the light staring down at me to once again face the dead place.

Sadly I realize I'm quite honestly more comfortable down here than balancing up on the cliff, constantly surrounded by those other voices. Nobody expects things from me here. My shame is only my own down here. I sigh, accepting the familiar sense of defeat and begin to listen to the unthinkable words of the voice from the dead place. I begin to forget about my other life of balancing on the edge of the cliff and look for somewhere to rest my eyes. My energy is depleted, and it's too hard to stay awake. As the dead place senses its victory, it begins to whisper wickedly about hopelessness, loneliness, shame, guilt, and defeat. An old movie projector noisily jumps to life. I watch with dread as images of every failed job, business, friendship, and relationship begin to flicker by on the wall. On the opposite wall, I cringe as I see a parade of faces of the people I've let down in my lifetime. I feel ashamed and cry out from the sharp stab of hate I have for myself. Like a broken record, I begin to attack myself. If I love them, why do I let them down? Why am I like this? Why can't I be normal? Why is this so hard for me? I realize with panic that I don't have the answers. I'll never have the answers, and my life will always be this mind-numbingly hard. My throat tightens, and I can't breathe. My heart responds by beating frantically as my stomachs pinches with tension and my hands start to shake. Gasping for breath, every movement becomes a struggle.

Remembering the words of the voice from the dead place, I slowly realize that I'm not strong enough (I must have been tricking myself into thinking I ever was strong) to endure this mental and physical torture for another second, let alone a lifetime. I can't fathom living through it. A person just cannot live that way. It's not even fair to ask them. I begin to relax, letting the dead place settle in my heart, a mere whisper away from my soul.

The ending always makes me giggle because it sounds so dramatic. You'd think that would be the end, huh? I mean, "a mere whisper away from my soul" surely sounds like death! Well, let me tell you, I have been in the dead place more times than I care to remember, and it hasn't killed me yet...and *I* haven't killed me yet. I have finally learned that when I'm there, my perspective is all wonky. I don't trust anything my brain tells me, because I know that the ol' translator isn't working so well...it's basically *opposite day* upstairs. I usually stay down for anywhere from two weeks to several months. My longest visit in the dead place was eight months, and it was ugly, but again, I made it out. The only way out is to climb, bloody fingernail by bloody fingernail, back to the top of the cliff to the designated post, teetering on the edge, knowing full well that I'll fall to the dead place again fairly soon and go through the entire nightmare again. It sounds bad and definitely like a shitty way to exist, but it's either that or I just kill myself. Think about it. If I killed myself, I would never have to wobble on the edge of the cliff or endure the eternal suffering of the dead place again. It's really a toss-up because all of my options sound so groovy! Gee whiz...how to choose, how to choose? My only problem with that whole *killing myself* malarkey is that I just can't imagine that my purpose in this world is to live a constant, daily struggle for thirty-odd years just to end it by gagging down some pain pills and crapping my pants while gasses escape from my butt with loud popping noises. That's not really what I had in mind by "going out with a bang." I want to see what this is all for. I want to see it through till the end. It's the only way I'll ever know how strong I truly am, what my gifts are, and how they'll contribute to humanity. Besides that, when it comes down to it, I'd much rather go through a lifetime of my own torturous angst than to put those that I love through the pain of my self-inflicted "going out with a fart" instead of a bang to the head.

Chapter 2

In the corner was a guitar, amp, and a microphone stand for his impromptu jam sessions of *Puff the Magic Dragon.*

I made my entrance into this gorgeous world on February 7, 1973. The world may have been gorgeous, but my entrance, um…not so much. In a hospital, on Keesler Air Force Base in Biloxi, Mississippi, my mom was sitting on a gurney, politely calling out to any nurse or doctor that might be walking by on the other side of the curtain. "I think I'm sitting on my baby's head!" She was alone, because the Air Force didn't find it necessary for my dad to leave work to witness the miraculous birth of his first child, and unlike the spalike atmosphere of the birthing suites of today, unless there was a slimy, bean-shaped head popping out of your vagina, you were on your own. A curious thing, whenever the "sitting on Stacey's head" story comes up, inevitably someone in the room asks, "So is that what happened to you?" I'm still trying to figure out if they are just trying to be funny or if they are seriously wondering.

As an Air Force family, we moved every two to three years. By my tenth birthday, I had lived in Mississippi, California, Japan, California again, Utah, and Kansas. My brother, Chris, joined our family in Okinawa. He and I absolutely loved moving, and leaving familiar cities didn't much matter because we always had each other. Being built-in best friends, we never had a hard time adjusting to new places or people. Different rooms, fine. Different friends, great. Different school, no problem. Different country, done.

Okinawa, Japan
Age 3

My parents had a hard time getting me out of my kimono and favorite cherry kicks.

My family parted ways in Utah after my parents' amicable divorce. They gave us the standard, "We *love* each other; we're just not *in* love." To be honest, it wasn't a huge, traumatic experience for me, and in some ways I feel guilty about that. Though, in my defense, they never fought in front of us, and I was used to my dad being gone for his job, sometimes in other countries, so this concept of divorce was just an extended temporary duty in my book, plus, that enabled us access to "Summer Dad." Every summer (until it became too testosterone-ish for me, as my brother got older), we would fly (or road trip back with our dad) to wherever he was stationed and spend a couple of months. Summer Dad would plan all these really great road trips and adventures, where inevitably (at least until he overtook me in size), my brother was squished in the hatchback of whatever sports car ("chick magnet") my dad was leasing at the time. I remember being sixteen and visiting him while he was stationed at Nellis Air Force Base in Las Vegas. At that time, he had a black Jeep CJ-7. He would let us take him to work in the morning and pick him up in the evening so my brother and I would have transportation to the community pool on base, which was, of course, *the* hangout. My brother and I were like rock stars when we pulled up. We made lots of friends and lots of memories thanks to that Jeep. I'd like to think we would have anyway, but we certainly didn't mind the extra help. Our dad always wanted our time with him to be really special, and his effort certainly paid off. I'll have those memories forever, which is hard to come by with this kooky brain.

Chick Magnet

This is my dad in just one of his "chick magnet" rides. I've never asked him if they actually got him any chicks, and frankly I don't want to know! Eww!

As the years went by, we got older and summers spent hanging out with friends became important. We saw our dad less, but we always stayed in contact. Sometimes we wouldn't hear from him for a couple of months, but never really thought anything of it. Now that I have kids and an amazingly wonderful stepmom (we call her Bonus Mom) that keeps my dad on track, we see them once or twice a year and every third Christmas. I'm not sure what my dad's version of this whole thing is, but for years he has told me that he doesn't want to end up on Oprah, defending himself while I tell her how he totally screwed up my life. What I think he doesn't realize is the fact that he fully expects me to be on Oprah for any reason at all is, in my opinion, part of what makes him such a good dad. He believes in me, and that's all I need.

After the divorce, my dad continued his military career in Wyoming, and my mom, with a new college diploma in hand, moved us kids, along with our dog and cat, to a small town in Kansas. As the new head of our household, she went to work for Boeing as a Logistics Engineer. That move would prove to be the catalyst for the end of my world as I knew it. Smiles, laughter, stability, and basic comfort would be making less of an appearance in the next phase of my life, replaced instead by fear, anxiety, stress, shame, guilt, and the occasional needless bruising.

While living in Utah toward the end of my parents' marriage, PJ showed up in our life. He was in some of my mom's college classes and they hit it off. PJ would take my parents flying in his small plane. I know what you're thinking, but trust me, I have asked both my mom and dad (who have always been honest, law-abiding citizens) if he caused the demise of their marriage, and they both said that it was over before PJ showed up. He ended up moving away while my parents' marriage faded away.

It was late one night, and my mom was pulling things out of the hall closet. My dad was already settled in Wyoming, and the house was up for sale. It looked kind of chaotic, and she's usually the epitome of calm, so I asked her what was going on. She said we were packing up the car and driving to Kansas where she had a job interview with Boeing. As I'm sure you know by now, I was instantly excited! Road trip! We got to make the drive again when, soon after, she was offered a position with the company. She packed us up and off we went. We were still driving the next morning when I asked her where we were going to stay. She asked me if I remembered PJ. I said I did. She then told me that PJ ended up getting stationed in Wichita, Kansas (Air Force, if you can believe it), and invited us to stay with him until we could get settled. I'm surprised to say that the earth didn't shake with foreboding doom after she finished her sentence. I didn't even think to ask any more questions. All I could think about was how bad I had to pee.

He lived in a tiny little house in a tiny little town outside of Wichita. It was what my brother and I referred to as a "grandma" house. It was painted brown and yellow with a wrought-iron rail poorly guarding the small, cement porch. There was a working set of train tracks not thirty feet from the house. In case you're wondering, you actually *can* get used to a freight train going through your front yard. It got so I wouldn't even hear it as it moved through our little town, blowing its agitated horn. The house had a working well in the back-yard with an actual bucket that hung from a rope. Whenever we pulled the bucket up, tiny frogs would leap back to the safety of the bottom of the well. The well wasn't the only dank thing around. As soon as you walked into the house, a faint, musty odor would reach your nose and hold on until you left. It had dingy brown carpet that practically moved on its own, due to the high volume of fleas that inhabited it. PJ's décor consisted of license plates from all over the country that neatly marched across the walls. In the corner was a guitar, amp, and a microphone stand for his impromptu jam sessions of "Puff, the Magic Dragon." I'm sure he knew and played more songs, but that's the one that sticks out in my head. There was a wood-burning stove between the small living room and dining area. The dining room led to a closed-in porch, which was PJ's makeshift bedroom. There were two other small bed-rooms in the front of the house, off the living room. My room was on the right; my brother's was on the left. Mine had a window that overlooked the front porch. It was through that window that my best friend, Kelli, would see something that would send her running from my house scared out of her brain. This "grandma" house is where I ceased being a carefree kid. This is where a man named PJ chewed up my newly shrunken family and dis-gustedly spit us out like we were the brown-tinged mucus he vehemently launched out of his infected sinuses every fifteen minutes. This is where I was unknowingly introduced to my AD(H)D and the consequences that came from having it.

I don't know exactly when PJ began to dislike my brother and me. My brain doesn't seem to be wired for many details. I remember in college, when I first attempted to paint with oils, it looked like a drunken kindergartner got hold of my canvas. I didn't expect too much from myself (never do) but I remember being completely *shocked* at how bad it actually was. To make it look artsy, I smoked some of my boyfriend's weed and came up with a bunch of words and sayings to write all over it with a Sharpie. The painting still ended up terrible, but in my *highly creative state*, I came up with a quote that still to this day embodies my kooky world: "It's either hot or cold…there's no lukewarm for me." In case you aren't following my nonlinear way of thinking, the details in life are what I consider to be lukewarm. Burn my eye sockets or freeze my limbs off…whatever you can do to keep me stimulated, just keep me away from that creepy *lukewarm* feeling, that eerie feeling of empty, nothingness. Blech.

I do recall some fun times with PJ…well, maybe two or three or one. There were those few times he pulled us behind his car on our toboggan through the snowy neighborhood street. I also remember a couple of nights when he did doughnuts in the icy parking lot of the grocery store down the street. We loved it. We would yell and yell and yell, and he would laugh and laugh and laugh. Looking back, I realize now it was all part of his plan to destroy the universe. OK, maybe not destroy the universe, but he was playing a game, and I'm pretty sure my mom was the prize. As a mom now, I know that the quickest way to my heart is through my kids (and of course, my stomach).

My mom's job at Boeing required her to travel. At this point, her and PJ's "friendly" relationship had blossomed into something more (well played, asshole), so it was expected that he would watch over us while she traveled. The same effect could be had by shooting a loaded gun in a steel room. He didn't have kids, he didn't understand kids, and he just plain didn't like 'em. As you have probably guessed, that didn't bode well for the two of us.

There were very strict rules in the house. I'm sure (if you're psychotic) you'll be able to see the importance of enforcing them and why brute force was necessary. Here are the top three things that meant your pants went around your ankles, your face went into the bed, and PJ and his angry red face unleashed all of the fury that pulsed through his veins due to the disappointment of his own crappy existence.

1. Forgetting to turn off the light in our bedroom.
2. Forgetting to hang up our toothbrush after use.
3. Losing the house key we were forced to wear around our necks.

Forgetting, forgetting, and losing. You could pretty much bet that I would be in one or the other compromising situations on a weekly, if not daily, basis. I knew this. PJ knew this. He was an asshole, but he wasn't a dummy. He was guaranteed a rage-release party at least once a week, and my butt always had the Golden Ticket. Pretty soon it got to the point where he was barely able to conceal his excitement at the prospect of pounding on me and my brother. He nicknamed me Spacey and thrived on what that meant for him. I probably aged twenty years that first year we lived with him. My world was not carefree. My world was walking through a field of landmines, taking cover when I tripped one, then stitching on the limbs that had just been blown off. The physical pain wasn't fun, but the mental torture was unbearable. At school, when lunch period ended, the knot in my stomach would begin to form. *Did you turn off your bedroom light?* I don't know…I think so, but I don't remember. *Well, what about your toothbrush? Did you hang it up?* I don't know…I don't remember that either. *Touch the dirty string hanging from your neck; is the weight of the key still pulling it down, or have you already lost it?* It's still there. *But, what have you done that you don't know about yet?* I don't know…I don't know! That was the thing—we never really knew which direction it was going to come from, but we knew we would find out shortly after 3:15 p.m., when the final bell rang.

I once read an article that claimed AD(H)D is genetic, yet there are also environmental triggers, including (but not limited to) chemicals, foods, toxins, and physical abuse. Apparently, in an abusive situation where stress hormones, activated by your fight-or-flight response, are released on a consistent basis, your brain creates a new "baseline," where your new normal of functioning is now you functioning with a higher level of anxiety. Basically, constant anxiety and fear train your brain to consistently stay in that fight-or-flight mode. You can imagine how that might affect a person's quality of life.

As a mom, I am always conscious of how my words and actions might affect my kids. If I yell at them, is that abuse? If I pop them on the butt to get their attention, is that abuse? Will *they* have *me* on Oprah? I finally read an article that assured me that I am actually not the monster mom that I envisioned. I'll give you the nuts and bolts (at least how it stuck in my mind). It said unless you are a parent that intentionally doesn't give medicine or medical attention to your sick child, laughs when your child gets hurt, withholds food and water for punishment, keeps your child in a small dog crate or corner of a room for weeks at a time, and so on, you're not abusive. I guess PJ didn't read the same article.

My elementary school was about a half mile down the street from the house, which enabled us to easily walk back and forth. I remember one night in the gym, standing on the elevated platform in the center of the basketball court. We were having a choir concert, and all of the parents were seated on the bleachers. My face felt like it was on fire, and the muscles in my lower back and legs were beginning to ache. I began feeling light-headed, and sat down right in the middle of a song to avoid passing out ("Don't lock your knees when you're up there, kids, or you'll fall face first"). I was too embarrassed to leave the platform, so I sat hidden behind the kids standing on the first level down from me. By the time the concert was over, I was so miserable, I could barely walk. With my eyes glossy and face burning red with fever, I was finally able to find PJ, my mom, and my brother through the crowd of proud parents. To my surprise, PJ was smiling, though the observation quickly left my mind as the aching in my muscles increased from the strain of walking. My mom felt my head and said, "You're burning up; let's get you home." Obviously, the absence of her daughter from the platform didn't escape her attention. Unfortunately for me (and gleefully for PJ), they had walked to the school, which meant we had to walk home. I honestly thought I would never make it. That night, PJ was in an exceptional mood, almost giddy. When we were about halfway home, as he started speaking to me, I realized why.

PJ: Well, I'm afraid I have some bad news.

Me: What?

PJ: You forgot to hang up your toothbrush.

Me: Oh….*He won't punish me when I'm so sick…will he?*

PJ: I understand you aren't feeling well, but when you break the rules, you still have to get punished. I just want to let you know that you'll be getting a spanking (that's what he called it) when we get home.

I'm not really sure what my response was to him, but that is the first time I can recall wanting to lie down and die…truly wanting to die. When you're a kid, you don't know that things can change. You think the rest of your life will be like the horrible day you're having. Much to my mom's disapproval, I did get the spanking when I got home, and it was every bit as bad as you can imagine one would be when you're in the midst of a fever, chills, and aching muscles. I didn't have the energy to cry and writhe around, so I just took it. I think it may have taken some of the fun out of it for PJ, though after it was over and I was lying on my pillow with hot tears running down my fevered face, I remembered his creepy smile at the school and knew things were beginning to escalate.

Chapter 3

I couldn't help being disappointed by his exit. It was utterly boring and anticlimactic. If I were him, I would have at least trashed the house or shot a pistol at the ceiling for dramatic effect.

It was late in the day, and my brother and I were playing in the front yard when PJ called us into the house. We could tell he was pissed because his face was almost purple. He told us to get our asses in the kitchen and promptly started stabbing the air in the direction of the open oven. "Who did this?" Chris and I looked at each other blankly. We didn't know what he was talking about. There was some sort of pie on the rack. Was he asking us if we baked the pie? Our blank stares pissed him off even more, so he began to almost yelp in fury. "*I said who in the hell did this?*"

I went out on a limb and replied matter-of-factly that neither my brother nor I were responsible for baking the pie, as we had both been outside playing. I was serious. He took it as sarcasm and went apeshit. "Get in your rooms now. I'll be there in five minutes to ask you again who messed up this pie. If you don't give me an answer, you'll get a spanking until you do!" I was rushing out of the kitchen but looked quickly enough at the pie to notice that a handful was missing. He came to the hall between our rooms and asked my brother first and then me if we had any part in the destruction of his precious Mrs. Smith's store-bought apple-fucking-pie. Unfortunately for us, we both shook our heads. To make an ugly story short, he would come into our rooms every fifteen or twenty minutes to repeat the question. If we repeated our answer (no), we would receive another spanking. I'm not sure how long he did that—over two hours, I would say. Eventually his hand got sore, and he turned to wooden and plastic utensils, switching to one after the other broke. Neither my brother nor I ever admitted to messing up the pie. We just took the spankings. We were little kids; we had no choice. It was that unfortunate incident that my best friend was witness to after skipping up on the porch to see if I could play. She glanced in my windows and saw PJ in action. I was literally unable to sit for a couple of days and had bruises from the middle of my back to the back of my thighs. She didn't tell me she had seen this for months afterward because she was so embarrassed for me.

I remember when my mom found out. It was less than a week later, and I was having one of my quarterly allergic reactions to something unknown that would manifest as a rash starting on my ears and slowly begin creeping over my whole body. The only way to stop the reaction was to go to the hospital and get a shot of Benadryl in the butt. The condition of my butt that day did not bode well for PJ. It was another Air Force hospital, where the nurse asked me to lower my pants. She left the room as I was doing so. I remember the look of shock on my mom's face when she saw my marble-patterned backside. PJ's eyes got wide (why would he look so surprised at the aftermath?), and he immediately went into true abuser mode. He was in a panic to get the story straight before the nurse came back to give me my shot at ground zero. At the same time, I was trying to explain to my mom what really happened in a three-second version of the events. When PJ exclaimed that, if asked, I was to tell the nurse that I fell while roller-skating, my mom almost roared with anger, "You will certainly *not* tell her you fell down while you were roller-skating. You tell her the *exact* truth!"

PJ's concern was getting kicked out of the Air Force for child abuse, and my mom didn't give a flying fuck. For the first time since PJ had added his chaos to our calm, I saw a glimmer of hope. My mom was witness, and the bruising was so bad there was no way the nurse could not notice. I couldn't wait for her to ask me so I could tell her what he did to me and my brother. It would finally stop. The Air Force would *make* it stop! Hooray! The nurse walked back into the room with the syringe of Benadryl and my future in her hands. She navigated around the bed, lifted the back of my shirt, inserted the needle in the midst of the rainbow bruising, let my shirt fall, and threw the needle in the container. "This should kick in soon, and the rash will begin to go away." Then she left. There was no questioning as to how I obtained such painful marks on my ten-year-old body, no military police storming in in disgust to arrest PJ for beating up innocent kids, and no reason for PJ to come up with his abuser lies. That nurse did the worst thing she could have ever done—she did absolutely nothing, which left us at square one. I'm not sure how my mom took care of that with PJ privately, but whatever she said, it didn't work.

Less than a year after moving from Utah, PJ, my mom, my brother, myself, Lady (our black Lab), and the newest member of the dysfunctional family, Walter (a Peking duck), packed up and said good-bye to the grandma house. If you're wondering what happened to my cat, join the club! After Ernie decided to have PJ's parakeets for lunch, the last I saw of her was when PJ picked her up and launched her across the yard like a furry torpedo. Not only that, but because *my* cat ate *his* birds, *I* was expected to sell his shitty, used, $9.99 bird cage like a traveling salesman up and down Main Street. He made me leave index cards with the bird-cage information at every business in town. It looked like *I* was the crazy one! I frantically looked for Ernie for a couple of days before PJ smugly informed me that he had taken her to a "farm" to enjoy the remainder of her life. I was smart enough to understand that *I took her to a farm* meant *I wrung her neck.*

Lady & Walter

Lady patiently letting Walter nip at her face for some beak kisses. Having a duck was a valid excuse for any strange marks that happened to land on my neck.

A girl (me) and her duck.

We ended up in a duplex on the west side of town in Wichita, Kansas. This place was slightly less depressing than the last, and thankfully the carpet wasn't infested with fleas. My bedroom was in the basement. My window looked out to a basement patio with stairs leading up to the backyard, which in the future would allow for me to "escape" both mentally and physically from the chaotic environment inside. I spent a lot of time in that room, especially the northeast corner. You see, after a while the "spankings" weren't getting the response PJ so desperately wanted. Don't get me wrong—he continued to spank—he would never give that up, but he started getting creative. He started adding punishments on to the spankings, like he was composing a twisted melody that played continuously in his ugly mind. I can see his psychotic wheels turning now: "OK, first, I'm going to beat their asses senseless, and then, hmmm…oh…I know! I'll ground them…but I have to do it in the sickest way possible, so I'll ground them to a small corner of their bedroom. I'll make them face the corner, and I'll give them a schedule of what time they can drink and use the bathroom. Their food will be brought to them. They'll be like prisoners. But is that *sick* enough? Hmmmm…aha! I'll ground them to a corner of their room, with a schedule for drink and restroom breaks, *for a month at a time*! Brilliant! Mwahahahaha!" Yep, you read correctly. I was grounded to the *corner* of my room for a month, on more than one occasion. *Why*, you ask? The usual: forgetting, forgetting, and losing.

Restriction to the corner of our room wasn't the only beauty he came up with. One night, my brother and I were being punished for some lame reason or another, and PJ thought it would be a good lesson to make us stack some firewood. I know you're thinking, "Nothing wrong with a little elbow grease. Hard work will put hair on your chest." I agree. I think hard work is important, but for PJ it wasn't about teaching us life lessons; it was about torture. He filled the entire walk-out basement patio with firewood. The wood was stacked so deep that it covered up my window. When my brother and I stood on the wood, we were standing level with the backyard. We had to dig through over six feet of firewood to clear a space to begin stacking the wood. We did that by burrowing through and throwing the wood across the patio as more wood would inevitably slide down to take its place. The job seemed impossible and endless. We were still stacking the wood well into the night. I remember at one point asking PJ what time it was, and finding it was almost 10:30 p.m. Initially, he said we couldn't come in until we were finished with the stacking. It was after 1:00 a.m. when he finally let us into the house. We still had more than half left to stack, which he so kindly let us resume the next morning. I'm not sure whether to feel ripped off or thankful, as I only got one, unfortunately placed nipple hair out of that whole ordeal!

I can count on one hand the number of people that have heard my stories about PJ; inevitably I am always asked the same two questions. The first is, "Did he ever *touch* you?" The answer is *no*, thank God, no. But I do remember a particularly gross experience. Let me set it up for you so you can understand. PJ had no shame. He peed with the door wide open for the whole world, or at least those in my house, to see. I couldn't stand it; he wasn't my dad (though I laugh to imagine my dad peeing with the door open…it would never happen), and it embarrassed me, until later my humiliation turned to anger (then anger became a significant part of me and ended up sticking around for two decades). I was thirteen, and fear of PJ was being replaced with disgust. One evening PJ was in the tub. He called me into the bathroom where the door was (gasp, shock, surprise) open. I'm not sure what the conversation was about, but the next thing I know, I was sitting inside the tub with my legs hanging out. He had pulled me in, fully clothed! I squirmed trying to get out of the tub, without touching an inch of PJ, but he grabbed me and held me in. He told me to just take off my clothes and take a bath, since I was already in there. I was in a panic and told him no. After a couple of attempts to wiggle out of the bath, PJ let me know in a not-so-nice tone that it wasn't a choice. I was to take off my clothes and finish my bath with him. I did what I was told, but I was furious. If the shared bath isn't creepy enough, he then made me stand in front of him, while he sat in the tub, and shampoo his hair! Ewwww! Even at thirteen, I was fully aware that he was showing me who was in control. It wasn't about being sexual toward me; it was about controlling me. I also knew that he only felt the need to flex those muscles (excuse the analogy) because that control was beginning to slip, and he knew it.

The other question I'm asked is, "Did he ever hurt your mom?" To my knowledge, no, I never witnessed anything, nor has she told me otherwise. I have asked her on more than one occasion about waking up to see a huge black and purple spot circling her eye. Her response then and now is that she grew faint and passed out, face to table. I choose to believe what she says, because she has always been an extremely honest and sincere person, and she has no reason to lie. We both know what our life was like, and it goes without saying that he mentally and emotionally abused her—maybe that was enough to satisfy his sick mind.

With the addition of Walter came the added responsibility of taking care of another pet, which fell on my shoulders. For what it's worth, I have never considered taking care of animals to be a chore. I thoroughly enjoy the privilege of being loved by these creatures, and give back to them by providing warmth, shelter, food, and lots of hugs, nuzzles, and kisses, including duck beak kisses. Unfortunately for me, with Walter came a cage, with the cage came a lock, and with the lock came a key. Another key for me to keep track of, another reason to beat me if I lost it, and lose it, I did…over and over and over again. More often than not, PJ was the one to find it. I became obsessed with keeping track of the key. I would go to the hook hanging next to the fridge multiple times a day to make sure it was still there. You can imagine already the amount of times I visited the bathroom to make sure my toothbrush was still hanging, or my bedroom to make sure the light wasn't on like a beacon, beckoning to the Great Hurter o' the Asses. To my dismay, even with all of the double-, triple-, quadruple-checking, inevitably the duck key would always disappear, and I would always blame myself for the consequences. Turns out, I should have given myself more credit and PJ less—way less.

The mystery of the vanishing duck key was solved one day when I was looking for something in the cabinets above the fridge. I always put important items in safe places and then forget where the safe place is, so sometimes I just have to search the entire house. As I was digging through old appliance warranties, my heart jumped when I saw something familiar fall out from behind some old phone books…the duck key! I would recognize that key anywhere, as PJ had attached it to a mayonnaise lid to keep me from losing it. What was the duck key doing in the cabinet above the fridge? I guarded that thing like a precious gem; there was no way I would carelessly throw it in the back of a rarely used cabinet! My heart flipped and stuttered a few times as I realized the enormity of what I had discovered. The key was not lost. It was never lost (well, maybe a few times). It was hidden! PJ hid the key so he would have an excuse to beat my ass and send me to the corner of my room for a month! Bastard! By this time, PJ's poop no longer smelled like roses to my mom, and I felt comfortable sharing my discovery with her. The look on her face when I showed her the key confirmed everything for me. I was right. Something had changed. My mom had stopped being the referee and picked a side. PJ was now the opposing team. Three against one. Game on.

A month or so after the duck key incident (by the way, it never disappeared again…fancy that), I came home to find a bunch of boxes stacked in our living room. By that time, PJ was a commercial pilot and usually had three- or four-day trips. The time when he was gone was an unbelievable relief, but we paid for it dearly when he was home. His schedule was on the fridge, and probably the only thing in my life I had bothered to memorize. The days I knew he was coming home were met with fear and anxiety. If he was expected home at night, I would lay in bed until he got home just to hear the tone of his voice to know what kind of day tomorrow would be. If he was in a bad mood, I would be so scared he would yank us out of bed to punish us that I would lay in my bed on my back, arms to my side, stiff as a board, inevitably waking up the next morning in the exact same position. I was never relaxed. Awake or asleep, I was terrified.

As I walked into the living room, my mom stepped from behind a stack with her trusty little packing tape tucked in her waistband (that lady is so efficient!).

Me: What are you doing?

Mom: Packing PJ's stuff.

Me: Why?

Mom: Because I told him he has to move out.

And that is seriously all I remember of that conversation. You would think it would have been the most important moment in my life up to that date, and well worth remembering, but I don't. One thing I do recall is PJ coming home from his trip to all of his crap packed in boxes in the front room. He couldn't believe she had the gall or the balls to kick him out. I knew she did. My mom is the sweetest woman you know, and she'll tolerate a lot, but when she hits her limit, the shit hits the fan, and it did. He came up to my mom demanding to know why his stuff was in boxes, and I swear that lady grew six inches (she's just a little thing), gained a hundred pounds of muscle, developed red glowing eyes, and spit nails in between her words. I high-tailed it downstairs to take cover. About thirty minutes later, PJ stomped into my room, and I found it absolutely impossible to feel fear. I only felt victory, and I'm pretty sure it was written all over my smirking face. He looked at me, lowered his red, sweaty face two inches from mine, and venomously spat out, "I hate you. I hate you so God-damned much, and I just want you to know that no matter where you go, or where you are, there will *always* be someone that hates you...*always*," and stomped out. Womp. Womp. Womp. *Really? That's it? That's all you have, you Bates Motel motherfucker*! I couldn't help being disappointed by his exit. It was utterly boring and anticlimactic. If I were him, I would have at least trashed the house or shot a pistol at the ceiling for dramatic effect. *Loser.*

Chapter 4

It wasn't hard to imagine myself screaming something juvenile like "ball fart sucker" while stabbing PJ in the eye with some tweezers.

Some time after that, my friend Danele and I were seeing a movie. It was snowing as we walked out of the theater, and I got really excited. I was sixteen with a new license, and I couldn't wait to drive in the snow. This is a good example of my lack of regard for safety. I get excited in situations when most would be hesitant, if not a little nervous. As we reached the parking lot, I saw a familiar car pull in and head for my parked car. My stomach literally dropped to my feet, and I felt like I was going to throw up. It was PJ, and he had parked, waiting for us. As we walked up, he smiled and said "Hi. Your mom was worried about you driving in the snow, so I told her I would follow you home." I smiled back. Isn't it funny how manners kick in even when facing your archenemy?

I just stood there, with a stupid smile on my face, said, "Oh, cool," turned around, and got into my car. My friend was more than familiar with PJ's antics, and was just as freaked out as I was. We hardly spoke on the way home. She asked me if I wanted to spend the night at her house, but I didn't want to. I wanted to do battle. Slowly, I felt an intense anger begin to fill my chest. My heart started galloping, and my hands were shaking. I'm not sure if I was more mad at PJ or my mom. How dare him! How dare her! When we got to my house, my friend got into her own car with another offer of a slumber party, as PJ pulled up beside us and turned off his car. Again, I declined her and went into the house. I walked in the door and straight to my room. I was abso-fucking-lutely furious. I felt like a caged, wild animal. I wanted to punch holes in my wall, and kick the dresser over. I wanted to be destructive. I was afraid if anyone knocked on my door, the scream I was holding in my chest would rip out of me, and I wouldn't have control over my words or actions. It wasn't hard to imagine myself screaming something juvenile like "ball fart sucker" while stabbing PJ in the eye with some tweezers.

Feeling like I was going to obliterate my room or a grown man's sight, I opened my window and climbed out into the cold, snowy night. I didn't know where to go, but I couldn't stay there. I could not believe it. I just could not imagine my life that way again. I knew I would never survive a life with PJ sprinkled in. I was more worried about what I would do to myself than what PJ would do to me. The vision of me at the duplex, sitting on my bathroom sink facing the mirror with a razor blade, slowly drawing lines in my face and arms was just too vivid. I never made big cuts. They were always very thin and noticeable to only me, unless you looked really close. At the time, I had absolutely no idea why I did that; I just knew it made me feel better. A couple of years ago, I came across the term "cutting." I couldn't believe that teenage girls were cutting themselves like I used to do, and that there was a name for it—not a very creative name, but a name nonetheless! C-U-T-T-I-N-G...

Injuring yourself on purpose by making scratches or cuts on your body with a sharp object—enough to break the skin and make it bleed—is called cutting... cutting is a way some people try to cope with the pain of strong emotions, intense pressure, or upsetting relationship problems. They may be dealing with feelings that seem too difficult to bear, or bad situations they think can't change. (kidshealth.org)

These days, you just Google the term, and all of this wonderful information will come up to help you understand why and what to do. Back then, I just thought I was nuts!

As I was standing in the snowy yard, I made the decision to go down the street to Bob's house. He met my mom at our neighborhood picnic, and I adored him from the start. He had two boys, one my age and one two years older. Bob had been coming around the house more lately, which is another reason I was so incredibly angry about this new PJ development. I knew she really liked Bob, and I knew Bob really liked her, so why in the hell would she ever let crazy-ass PJ back into the picture? As I stood ringing the doorbell, I noticed there was no light coming from inside, and sadly came to the realization that Bob wasn't home. He was probably on a trip, as he was *also* a pilot (my mom said that was almost a deal breaker when she met him at the picnic). I crossed to the other side of the street, and sat on the curb facing his dark house. I began to cry. It was one of those quiet nights where the moon was so bright I could see each and every snowflake as they floated to the ground. I was on the curb, feeling sorry for myself for about ten minutes before I saw PJ's car turn the corner heading from my house toward me. I could see the silhouette of two people, which meant my mom was also in the car, which meant they were looking for me, and I was busted. *Fuck them.* They pulled up in front of me. I didn't even give them the chance to roll down a window, before I sighed heavily, rose to my feet, and started heading back to my house. I heard them turn around in the snowy street, and the tires crunching the snow as they followed me. At that point, I didn't care how much trouble I was in—as far as I was concerned, they could have tied me behind the car and dragged me home. Nothing could be as bad as a future with PJ in it.

I walked into the house and straight to my room. I thought my life was over, which at sixteen, is not uncommon. I heard a car door close in the driveway. Hmmm. Only one? I heard the whine of PJ's car backing up. Carefully, I peeked out through the blinds to see his taillights flash as he headed out of our cul-de-sac. I knew my mom would be heading for my room, and I wasn't wrong. There was a surprisingly soft knock at my door. My mom poked her head in, and asked if I wanted to talk. I broke down and told her everything that was going through my head. I don't think I stopped for twenty minutes before she finally understood where I was coming from and what possessed me to slip out of my bedroom on a snowy night (I was caught when my friend called the house to make sure I was OK).

It turns out that PJ was only there picking up some items that he had been storing in our basement. When my mom had expressed concern for me after it began snowing, PJ had offered to drive to the theater to make sure we got home safe—because we all know that PJ was "concerned about my safety and well-being." It turned out that PJ wasn't just coming to get things out of the basement like my mom thought. He had other things in mind, like *reconciliation*! A few weeks (and apparently multiple phone calls) later, Danele and I were pulling into the cul-de-sac when we saw PJ's car in the driveway. We both inhaled sharply and stopped the car on the street. PJ was leaving something in the door. We looked at each other, started laughing (looked like an adventure to us), and quickly drove past while his back was still turned. About ten minutes later, we inched by the entrance again. PJ's car was gone, so we turned and pulled into the driveway. There was a note on the front door.

My mom was on a business trip, but when she called to check in that night, I told her about the note. She had me read it to her. I don't remember exactly what it said, but a part still stands out in my head. He said he had changed. He wanted my mom to be the queen, and my brother and me to be the prince and princess. He was going to treat us like *royalty*. My mom exhaled sharply when I read her the note, and mumbled something about "too little, too late," and it was, as that was the last of PJ.

My mom heard through mutual friends over the years that PJ was married and had a couple of kids. When she relayed it to me, I was sick to my stomach for days imagining those kids and their life with him. A couple of years ago, I was seeing an ayurvedic practitioner. In Ayurveda, like other old and wise medicinal traditions, they believe in treating the mind, body, and soul. It took a long time for the doctor to convince me that burying my feelings about PJ and the situation was not me being strong like I had thought, but actually quite weak and unhealthy. So in order to let those feelings out, he had me write a letter to PJ. I wrote the letter, which was honestly a hell of a lot easier than I thought it would be. I started off politely in the beginning, but by the middle I was tossing off f-bombs like nobody's business. It was actually very therapeutic for me, so much so that I decided PJ needed to read it. I paid $14.95 on the Internet for PJ's address at the time. I had a plan that I would mail it to a friend in another state, where she would mail it for me, so PJ wouldn't be able to tell where I lived. Before I mailed it, I wanted my mom to read it and give me some feedback. We were sitting on the patio of Starbucks when she read the letter. After reading it, she told me if I wanted to mail it I could, but that she preferred that I didn't. She told me she was afraid it would set him off, and he would do something bad. I truly thought she was kidding when she said that, and I laughed. After all, my mom is about as far from hysterics and drama as you can get. She said she was serious, and with him possibly still being a pilot, it gave him easy access to the whole country. She freaked me out, so I decided that writing it was therapy enough, but it wasn't until that conversation that I realized just how volatile and dangerous our situation had been. So, getting back to the environmental triggers for AD(H)D, for my situation, it's kind of like the chicken or the egg thing…did the AD(H)D trigger the abuse, or did the abuse trigger the AD(H)D? At this point, it doesn't really matter, because at the end of the day, my friend's favorite saying comes to mind: "It is what it is." No matter how that experience changed me, good or bad, *I'm* what I have to work with, and I can only be the best version of me. With every fiber of my being, I believe I was meant to experience that situation in order to grow and learn, so I don't hold grudges toward any parties involved. All is forgiven. Lessons learned. Life goes on. There's even a saying, "Resentment is the act of stabbing yourself repeatedly in the heart with a knife, hoping the other person dies." Sounds painful, fruitless, and just plain inefficient!

Section Two:
School Dazed & More Than Slightly Confused

"*Everybody is a genius. But if you judge a fish by its ability to climb a tree, it will live its whole life believing that it is stupid.*"

—Albert Einstein

Chapter 5

He was old, slow, and boring, and nothing brings out the ornery in me more than that.

Not long after being diagnosed with Adult AD(H)D and figuring out exactly how much of an impact it had on my past, present, and future, I went through a bit of a mourning period for my "lost" life. I found myself scrutinizing significant (and insignificant) moments in my time and studying them piece by piece, layer by layer, trying to figure out if my life wouldn't have somehow been different (better) if I would have just been normal. These thoughts often drift through my mind when I think about my time in school (especially since my daughter started kindergarten last year). If I had a dime for every time I heard, "If you would only apply yourself" from a teacher, I would be writing this book from a cabin in the Oregon mountains instead of from my crumpled, unmade bed, sweating my ass off in the inescapable Texas heat while a weed eater whines outside! Shut up! I can't think!

We were living in San Bernardino, California, when I began kindergarten. A month or so after school started, my teacher pulled my mom aside and made a suggestion. She thought I would be a good candidate for a new school that had opened for "high achievers." The downside would be that I would have to get bussed (which I was more than excited about, even if my mom wasn't), and this program was all-day, whereas the norm for kindergarten back then was half-days. At this point, I had been at home with my mom for the entire five years of my life, so somehow I doubt *all-day* kindergarten was considered a "con" on her part, and she agreed to let me go. It was exactly what I needed. I thrived in that environment…mostly because they really encouraged self-expression and curiosity.

When the bell would ring announcing recess, I always made a beeline for the gym bars. There were three gym bars, side by side, at different heights on the playground. My friends and I owned those bars. There was never any question as to who was going to be perched up there at recess. Though, I would have never been one to sit idly on my one-bar throne, chatting away… I had a purpose. Oddly enough (to those that know me, and have the pleasure of seeing my brain in action), there is always purpose in what I do; it's just sometimes harder for others to see the same connections I do. To *them*, I don't make sense, and *I* just don't have the attention span to explain what *they* can't see! Anyway, my purpose up there was to learn to defy gravity (in my five-year-old mind), by sitting on the bar, throwing myself back with my legs hooked and arms in the air, and do a full circle, finding myself perched up on the bar where I started…basically, only using the back of my knees to squeeze the bar to keep from falling off. It took me about two weeks' worth of recesses, but I finally did it without breaking my head open.

When I mastered that, the real challenge came. OK, now let me stop for a second and tell you that when I look back at this, I can't wrap my brain around the fact I had the balls and belief in myself to do what I did next. I think it's a good indication of what being conditioned to fit into a certain mold will do to a person if a person isn't allowed to be themselves. Most kids and adults with AD(H)D are constantly called out on behavior that isn't "normal." News flash, fuckers: we aren't your everyday kind of normal!

When someone is always told what to be, they never really know who they are or what their gifts are. Well, that is just not tolerated at the *School for High Achievers*, dammit! True story—when I decided that I wanted to put on a bar routine with the whole school as my audience, they were all over it and quickly set up the "show" for the next day. Twenty-two hours later, I felt no fear as I watched the kids, lined up by classes, taking their places on the grass around the gym bars. When everyone was seated, my teacher nodded, and I took my position on my favorite perch and began to execute my bar routine. I can't imagine that the whole shebang lasted longer than forty-five seconds, but by the round of applause from the kids and staff, you would have thought I'd just won an Olympic gold medal. And what's wrong with that? Sure, it's a little weird that I made the whole school watch me flip around, but it was more than that. It was the acknowledgement of my reaching the goal I had set for myself. Given, it was a weird goal, but a goal nonetheless, and I was on a good kiddie high for a few days after that. Months later, I had even better luck with the magic routine I put together. That time they let me go to each class and perform my routine for all of the kids. Again, I can't believe I put myself out there, but as cliché as it sounds—and I can't stress this enough—when someone tells you that you can do anything (as my parents did), then you truly believe you can do anything, and if you *believe* you can do anything, there is nothing you can't do. If you don't believe me, just try it for yourself; you'll be shocked at your own superpowers!

When we moved from San Bernardino to Layton, Utah, I had to say good-bye to my monkey bars, magic tricks, and the *School for High Achievers*. I was the poor-man's version of Harry Potter leaving Hogwarts, and for the three years spent in Utah before the divorce (as far as school and home goes), life was pretty uneventful. Since I had moved mid-year, I entered Lincoln Elementary as a kindergartner. It wasn't Hogwarts, but it wasn't half-bad, either. They had a cool after-school Spanish class that my parents put me in. Between that, Brownies, soccer, stealing and crashing my brother's bike, and charging the neighbor kids five cents to stare, wide-eyed, at the pheasant guts laid out in my wagon (the result of my Dad's hunting trips) as I wheeled it through the neighborhood (they got their money's worth…I always pointed out the large intestines), I was stimulated and happy, so there was no need for me to stir things up.

I wish I could say the same for the next nine years of my academic career. It pretty much went from sugar to shit when we made the move to Kansas. Again, I'm not sure what motivated me to go from star student to the kid the teachers drew the short straw for. Actually, that's not true at all. I do know why I became the student from hell—because I was bored out of my flipping mind, and my new teacher belonged in a retirement home. Mr. Jacobs had to have been in his seventies when I blessed him with my shenanigans. He was old, slow, and boring, and nothing brings out the ornery in me more than that. I'm either stimulated or dying inside, and my self-preservation is too strong to wither away. Unfortunately, Mr. Jacobs was an easy target to keep me stimulated. He had the patience of a crackhead mixed with the confusion of an old man. Watching him lose control was the highlight of my days, so much so that I began to plan in advance the mischief I was going to get into just to see him bluster and shuffle around the room. If that wasn't bad enough, I began to bring a tape recorder to record him reacting to my mischief, so I could listen to it and laugh later. You have to understand that, back then, the recorders were the size of a shoebox. To drag that around with me while keeping it hidden took a lot of effort on my part. What does that say about me? Don't answer that.

While Mr. Jacobs was my homeroom teacher, he was also my math teacher. It was he that introduced me to my aversion to math, which would haunt me to the last semester of college. I recall one day being in his math class (with the recorder on, of course) as he was explaining fractions. Apparently, my brain forgot to send him a memo on how it processes information, because I had no idea what he was talking about. Fortunately for me, I'm not afraid to tell someone that I don't understand what they're talking about. Trust me, I've had a lot of practice, and still do it almost daily. If you lose me in the beginning, I'll never catch up, and I hate feeling lost. I raised my hand and told him that I didn't understand the concept. He said to me, while illustrating on the board (Thank You from a visual learner), "If I had a pie, and I cut it into quarters, would you rather have one quarter or three quarters?"

Finally, he was explaining in a way that I understood! Thrilled, I looked back at him and said, "One quarter."

The frustration began to build in his face and his little-old-man hand started shaking as he brought the chalk to the board and started stabbing at his illustration.

His voice rose with the irritation. "No, you wouldn't. You would want three quarters!"

I looked at him indignantly and said, "No! I would want one quarter…I don't like pie!" All hell broke loose, and once again, I was "disrupting" the class. Sure, all the kids laughed when I said that, but I was being sincere with my answer. Mr. Jacobs didn't stop to think about the fact that my answer meant I finally understood the concept of fractions. He just wrote my name on the board and added a check mark while silently cursing me to the fiery depths of hell. Hello! I was already in my hell—his class! My only condolence was that I got it all on tape, and Kelli and I had some big belly laughs listening to it later.

Moving to Wichita and out of Mr. Jacob's class did nothing to change my newfound attitude about school. I had my role, and I knew how to play the part well. I was no longer in a gifted program, and had to find my own way of exercising my creativity. I found the best spot for that was the lunch room. The supervision wasn't as tight, and I was able to get away with more. For some reason that didn't keep me off of the wall (the wall is where the naughty kids had to stand at lunch and recess so the other kids could look at them with pity while they ran past to the playground). The wall was not enough motivation to keep me out of trouble. It sounds like I was bad just to be bad, but that really wasn't it. It was more of a curiosity thing with me. If I do *this*, what will happen with *this*? I still get into pickles to this day due to my never-ending curiosity.

One day, in the lunch room, I was obviously feeling "creative," and I began concocting a plan. My friend Brad was sitting directly across from me. Brad was a pretty good friend of mine, so my feelings toward him had absolutely nothing to do with what happened next; he was simply in the wrong place at the wrong time. I whispered conspiratorially to my girlfriend sitting next to me, and her eyes widened as she listened to my plan. She may have been scared, but she still agreed to participate. I filled my mouth with fruit punch and started making gargling noises as I held my throat. The entire table stopped eating to look at me and my overdramatic choking episode. On cue, my friend reached back and slapped me right between the shoulder blades, which fired off a gushing stream of lukewarm fruit punch from my mouth directly in the face of poor Brad. The table erupted into laughter, and I was once again escorted to the wall. I could barely contain my satisfaction or giggles standing up there. All I could think about was the shocked look on Brad's face as the red punch dripped from his nose. Thankfully, he was a laid-back kid with a wicked sense of humor, so he instantly forgave me, but truly, there's nothing like a job well done. The rest of my time in elementary school was peppered with standing on the wall, getting sent out in the hall, and visiting the principal's office, none of which did anything to deter me from my "creative" behavior.

In junior high, it was a different story entirely. There was one thing that motivated me to keep myself in check, and that was a paddle. Rumor had it that the paddle was riddled with drilled-out holes to make it even more painful, but I never (thank God) saw it first-hand. It's called corporal punishment, and it means the school is allowed to paddle you on the butt if you misbehave. I'm sure we can all agree that I had enough of that going on at home, so it was a huge motivator for me to keep my creativity in check. Don't get me wrong, I still caused trouble it just wasn't as obvious as the *old* trouble. A good example would be when, in history class, my friend, Lisa (whom we determined mere weeks ago is AD[H]D as well) leaned over her desk and whispered in my ear to *have a seizure*. I promptly agreed that it was a genius idea, and seconds later fell out of my desk to the floor, bucking around on the ground. Lisa dropped to her knees and started fanning my face with a sheet of paper, intentionally scraping my nose every time the paper passed from right to left and back. I nearly lost it with laughter, so I stopped bucking and looked around with a confused expression on my face. By that time the teacher was kneeling next to me on the floor, clearly in a panic. Lisa volunteered to take me to the nurse's office and our teacher readily agreed. We laughed the whole way down the hall on the way to the nurse and even pulled that stunt a few more times at the mall, only getting caught once and let off with a warning (she and I acted like that all the way through college). Other than that, the extent of my punishments consisted of having to crawl on the floor after school and pick up the hole-punches my math teacher scattered around the room for whatever small infractions I incurred due to my obvious "underachiever" math skills.

It seems that a lot of the pickles I have gotten myself into over the years are due to my inability to withstand injustice (at least what *I* consider to be unjust). Though, for the most part, I was able to keep my behavior in check (I was in pompon, and absolutely loved it, which gave me something positive to focus my energy on) during my freshman year, which we spent at the junior high, before they came up with the whole "middle school" thing. One of my best friends at the time became pregnant. We were fifteen, her parents were pretty religious; though well-loved by all of us kids, and it was quite scandalous at school. During gym (which was our pompon practice), as her body began to change shape, and before people began to suspect, she started to avoid "dressing up," which meant changing into those tight, navy-blue polyester shorts, and navy-blue and white striped shirts, otherwise known as *gym clothes.* The horizontal stripes on the shirt did nothing for her growing belly, and because not dressing up meant points docked, affecting our grade, everybody sported the horrendous outfits, so it probably did seem a bit fishy when she began to keep her street clothes on. With my strong sense of justice and humanity blaring like a bomb siren, I decided that I, too, would keep my street clothes on, to draw less attention from my growing friend (I can't say that it didn't feel great to be blatantly naughty). Now, this is where I screwed up. Our gym teacher knew she was pregnant, and had probably already agreed to her new gym fashion. I, on the other hand, didn't make the same deal, so every day it was announced that I was docked points. You know the other girls were looking at me, thinking, "You dumb shit…why don't you just put your damned gym clothes on?" I think I ended up with a C in that class, but I didn't care. In my mind, there was something bigger than their stupid rules (that statement right there is the epitome of my problems) and that was the emotional well-being of my friend. So, sue me! As a side note, that same friend was working as a nurse at the hospital the night that I arrived in labor with my daughter Willow. She saw my name appear on the patient list, came downstairs to the birthing floor (we hadn't seen each other in years), and was able to be present for the birth of my daughter along with Dave, my mom, Christa, Donya, Carrie, the lawn guy, and others—there were a whole lot of people that saw my privates that day…a *party in my pants*, if you will. I had forgotten about the whole *pooping on the table* thing, or I probably would have been a little more shy.

Chapter 6

It wasn't until that moment that I realized how much he protects me from my own weirdness.

My sense of fairness was not limited to the plight of humans, even back then. I was like a mini-PETA girl, without the red paint assaults. I was sitting in high school biology class one day, petting a Guinea pig named Bob. I used to love that class, because there was always some animal or another getting held as the teacher lectured from the front. Now, I'm one of those people that lives life totally in the moment. I would love to say it's because I'm so spiritually sound, but it's really because my brain is incapable of doing otherwise. There will be more on that later; my whole point is that it never crossed my mind as to why we had all of these Guinea pigs, mice, and hamsters. There were frogs and snakes, too. I guess I just thought it was for our viewing and/or petting pleasure. As I was sitting in my chair, petting Bob, my teacher announced that there was going to be a feeding after school. One of the snakes was going to eat an after-school snack, and we were invited to watch. Imagine the shock I felt when someone asked what the snake would be eating, and the teacher

·nodded in my direction, "Bob." There were gasps from most of the girls, and everyone looked at Bob cradled in my arms as I looked at the teacher.

"Are you being serious?" I said, looking from Bob to him and back to Bob. He (my teacher, not Bob) looked at me with a small tilt to his head, kind of like a dog does when they're trying to figure out something perplexing. I felt my heart take off, and my armpits began to itch like they were harboring a nest of fleas on each side (for some reason my pits always itch when I get a burst of adrenaline). My brain began to move at an impossible speed as I went through my options.

I began to formulate a plan, even as he answered, "Yes." I knew if my plan were to work, I couldn't make a big deal out of Bob's supposed fate. Twenty minutes later, class was over and as books were being closed and backpacks unzipped, I quietly tucked Bob into my jean jacket, and left with the flow of traffic...right out the front door of the school. I was stopped by security as I was driving out, and showed them Bob, explaining that he had been to biology with me, but I had to get him back home. They smiled and let me pass, and I giggled the whole way home. You may have noticed that I giggle a lot after my shenanigans. I think it's nervous energy, or maybe that's just what feeling *alive* can do to a person. As I've said before, if I'm not stimulated, I'm dying and depressed, so I do whatever it takes to make me feel alive, and if I'm saving the world at the same time, well that's just a bonus.

I was a good girl (that day), and returned to school immediately after dragging our old Guinea pig cage out of the garage and getting it nice and cozy for Bob in the basement. I even remembered to call my mom to warn her about the new addition to our family. Because it is almost impossible for me to tell a lie, I told her the truth about saving poor Bob from his painful fate. My mom is also a sensitive soul, and agreed to let Bob hide out (after a big looooooong sigh, as she knew what was ahead of me). It wasn't two hours later, when I was pulled out of my class to go to the principal's office. There stood the principal and two assistant principals. Of course I had already established relationships with them, so they knew me well. Even though I was a troublemaker, everyone knew my heart was in the right place, which sometimes saved my butt from the stricter punishments. Apparently they had already searched my locker (yeah, because I would just throw a Guinea pig in my locker and then go about my day), and they had a witness to the theft (a narc in biology!). Theft? It wasn't theft! I was saving, not stealing, him! I passionately told them the story of the 3:20 p.m. feeding and my primal urge to save poor Bob. In a weird turn of events, instead of a verbal lashing, they told me they were really proud of me for my actions and were sorry that I still had to be punished, because technically it was still a theft. Sounds good to me! I was walking on air. I didn't even care that I had to spend three days in the cave (which was really just a classroom and the in-school version of getting suspended), Bob was safe, the school had my back, and the kid that owned the Guinea pig in the first place (he had an owner?) decided that I could keep Bob, which meant he wouldn't have to face death by snake. Basically, in my book, life was A-OK.

As life goes, it didn't stay A-OK for long. I was kicked out of my history class, because I couldn't give the teacher a break. I loved calling attention to his inaccuracies and inconsistencies. In my teenager mind, he was so stupid and boring, I couldn't even tolerate him. I challenged him daily, just to get some juice going in that class. Bueller…Bueller…Bueller. As a result I ended up in summer school, which was not a foreign idea to me at all. I don't remember a summer where I wasn't in school, making up for whatever atrocities I had committed during the previous school year.

It wasn't just history that I found painful—it was math as well. That algebra never made a lick of sense to me. Calculating numbers and letters? What's wrong with you? Just use a calculator! Unfortunately, this was the '90s, and nonlinear teaching wasn't really a buzzword back then. Wait—it still isn't! What exactly *are* we doing with the nonlinear thinkers being taught in a linear classroom? Abso-fucking-lutely nothing, that's what! Those kids are shit out of luck, my friends, and that is something else that needs to change! I'll put that on my list of ways to change the world…*I know I have a pen around here somewhere*…anyway, if I'm not taught in a way I can actually understand,

I'll never get it. I'm lost from the get-go, never to catch up, and doomed to fail. Needless to say, over the years, the concept of algebra was never explained to me in that beautiful, chaotic, nonlinear fashion, so I never got it.

Because some of my classes were becoming a source of conflict, I began to "extend" my photography class by leaving school with some friends and going to different locations to take cool photos instead of stabbing my own heart with a pencil out of sheer boredom while trying to be present in a class I didn't like. I loved my photography class, so I gave it 200 percent. Yes, that's right, I'll give my heart, blood, and soul to anything I love, but if it's something that doesn't keep me stimulated and interested, forget it. It's not like I just pick and choose what I feel like doing; it's actually not up to me at all. If my brain decides something isn't interesting, it refuses to take any part in it. If I can't leave the situation physically, it will happen mentally. Off I go, inside this wacky mind, on another adventure that could keep me occupied for hours. I'm always shocked when someone claims that they are bored. I'm never bored! I can keep myself pretty entertained, and embarrassingly enough, I've been known to make myself laugh out loud. I've always thought of myself as having myself as a friend, kind of like I'm two people in one body. Hmm…I'm not sure if I should keep that last sentence in there. My husband would probably interject that it doesn't sound normal. He's kind of like the filter I lack, and lets me know what to say and what not to say to other people. An example of this is when I turned his tool shed into a yoga studio. After I was finished converting the shed (by attaching different fabrics to the framework with a staple gun and adding a lamp), he looked at all of the previous shed occupants in a pile in the corner of the garage, composed himself, and turned to me.

Him: You probably shouldn't tell anyone that you did this.

Me: What?

Him: Turned the shed into a yoga studio.

Me: Why not?

Him: [small exhale] Because it's not normal.

Me: What's not normal?

Him: Turning a shed into a yoga studio!

Me: What's wrong with that?

Him: I'm not saying anything is wrong with it. I'm just saying most people wouldn't do that.

Me: Oh. Wow...OK.

It wasn't until that moment that I realized how much he protects me from my own weirdness. He doesn't tell me that people think I'm weird, and he tries his best to make me appear less weird. Not in a "he doesn't accept for who I am" way...more like a "she has a hard enough time already" way. I find it sweet and very comforting.

As I was saying, thanks to my inspiring and motivating photography teacher, Mr. Strattman, and the creative subject matter, I adored photography, so I began skipping the classes that were boring and started taking photos with my friends Danele, Tonya, Alli, and Janelle, who also all loved photography. We would always go to the same nursing home on a beautiful property with fountains and greenery, where we would pose and take pictures, pose and take pictures. I felt so free and happy during those times. There was no one to answer to, no rushing from one class to another, and we were outside in the fresh air. Of course, as is always the case, it caught up with me. One day, I was sitting in English class when a school proctor quietly knocked on the door and proceeded to walk around our desks, heading to the teacher with a pink slip. A pink slip meant someone was being summoned from the class to the office for whatever reason. From my experience, nothing good ever came from a pink slip. Looking at my desk, my eyes began flitting up and back down again trying to gauge the pink slip situation going on at the front of the room. My worst fears were confirmed when the teacher glanced at me quickly after reading the note. Aww, man! "Stacey, you're needed in the office." Crap!

As I trudged the familiar path to the office, I went over in my head all of the possibilities for the summons. *Did they figure out that we had found the trap door that lead from the drama room to the auditorium? Do they know we actually use the trap door and tunnel into the auditorium when the lights go out on movie day in drama?* As a side note, we were almost caught in the act the day I fell down the stairs in the dark auditorium and ended up with a bloody nose and scraped knees and elbows. Thankfully the drama teacher was still asleep when we came out of the trap door, so my friend was able to get to the sink and swipe some paper towels so I could get the bleeding stopped before the lights came back on.

Once I was in the office, I flashed the brightest smile I could muster to the school secretary and gave her my slip. Unwavering, she told me to sit down and wait in one of the doomed chairs where the next step was inevitably sitting across from one of the principals getting an ass-chewing. As it was, I never had to visit an office that day, as all four principals came strolling in together. Great—my lucky day! They said hi and sort of stood there. I said hi and stood up as well. It was weird because we suddenly had a mini-meeting right there in the waiting area. All at the same time, they began to explain that there was "nothing they could do." "It's the school board policy." They "didn't have a choice." "Attendance is automatically reported to the district." "Thirty-six unexcused absences in a row." I just stood there watching every one move their mouths and tried to understand what they were telling me. I'm not sure when I finally got what they were saying, because I don't remember anything other than watching their lips move and feeling like I was in a movie. What it boiled down to was this: I had missed thirty-six days of class in a row. It sounds horrible, I know, but I didn't miss *every* class thirty-six days in a row, just those I didn't fancy going to. To make matters worse, I wasn't living within the proper city boundaries to attend my school, and hadn't been since we had moved a couple of years prior. My school had received word from the district that I was officially unenrolled from Northwest High.

My future was bleak, to say the least. I had two options. I could go to the rival Catholic school that my mom had frequently threatened me with, or I could go to the rival "country school," which was surrounded by a sheep farm. That's like holding a piece of crap in each hand and asking me which one I want to put in my pocket. Um…neither, fuck-you-very-much.

In the end, my fear of organized religion won out. Once, there was a lock-in advertised on the radio for junior high kids. It was being held at a local college, and my friends and I couldn't wait to go. As advertised, we were going to get to play games, dance, and swim all night long, just like the Lionel Richie song. In the end, the lock-in was actually a cleverly disguised Christian-conversion trap. We were made to sit in the auditorium and be "saved." We had to walk up to the front of the entire auditorium, in front of everyone, agreeing that we were, indeed, "saved." Then we had to file into these little cubicles where we had a one-on-one with a person who asked personal questions and shoved more Jesus down our throats. It was scary, humiliating, and traumatizing…no offense, Jesus. On top of that, they never even bothered to tell me what exactly I was being saved from! Thanks to those crazy Christians and their intentions that backfired, I wasn't about to head down the bullied into Jesus path, so I packed up my locker, said good-bye to my friends and teachers, and headed off to what I liked to refer to as *Triple-S*, the sheep shit school. I remember getting out of the car on my first day at the new school and literally gagging from the smell of livestock and poop. I should have taken that as a sign.

My days at Triple-S were not happy ones. I'm more of a male-energy guy's girl, so the guys liked to hang out with me, which meant the girls did not. That and coming from a rival school did not bode well for my popularity. It also didn't help that I had no need to establish any friendships in that school. I already had my friends. As far as I was concerned, going there was my punishment, so I dealt with it as such. Go in, pay my dues, and get out. After about seven weeks of classes, I became very depressed. Even though I had a tendency to skip a lot of my classes at Northwest High, I loved the social aspect of school. I had a lot of friends and I had known them for years. There was a certain basic comfort that was missing by changing schools, and it made me feel very unsettled. I missed my old friends, my old teachers, and my old school. When something is important to me, I can become extremely motivated to support its cause. At that point, the cause was myself, and I needed to get off my ass and make some changes ASAP. I called my old school and begged the principal to let me back in. He said it was out of his hands, but if I got approval from the school board, he would support their decision. I called the district, and they agreed to schedule an appeal based on the decision to expel me from the school. My mom went with me to the appeal and stood behind me as I faced the appellant committee. I was very nervous, but also very passionate as I explained why I wanted to go back to my old school. The committee came back with an approval to allow me to attend, on two conditions, which, if not met, would require that I leave immediately.

1. Absolutely zero unexcused absences.
2. Achieve honor roll status, and remain there until graduation.

Holy crap! That's a pretty tall order for a student with Cs and Ds that missed thirty-six days in a row! You know what though? It didn't matter. It meant so much to me to get that hated but needed structure and stability back that I was willing to do anything, even if it meant becoming a good student that attends class. After that, I never missed another day, and I was on the honor roll from that first new report card until the day I graduated. On the last day of school, my senior year, I was presented with a "Grizzly Award" for most improved attendance and grades. I don't think they will ever know how much that award meant to me. To receive the recognition for all of my hard work made everything worthwhile. It had been a while since I was recognized for anything remotely positive, and I will forever be grateful for that. In my heart of hearts, I believe receiving that award contributed greatly to the confidence that enabled me to feel like I could tackle college...a place known for their lax attendance policies.

Chapter 7

I learned about my penchant for physical comedy as a guest in a Mormon Church talent show.

My mom and Bob married in March of that year. Bob immediately moved to Florida to start a new flying job, and my mom stayed back to sell both houses and to get my stepbrother Ryan and me through graduation. My other stepbrother, Rob, had moved back to his original hometown the year before. After graduation, I stayed in Wichita, moving in with my boyfriend, Scott (whom I later became engaged and then unengaged to). Ryan headed off to wrestle at Ft. Hays, and my mom and brother finally hooked up with Bob in Florida. It was all a major adjustment for me. I had lost my family to geography and my dog, Lady, to old age within a few months of each other. I felt dead and empty inside for a long time. As a frustratingly independent soul, I trudged forward. The challenge of starting my own household was a perfect distraction, as it gave me something to focus on. I chose a college that allowed me to stay close to my boyfriend. I attended WSU in the fall. It only took one semester before I realized that I wasn't doing myself any favors by sticking around for someone else. I had moved from my family home into a home with a somewhat controlling boyfriend, and I was starting to feel that wanderlust itch that, to this day, kicks in every now and then. I needed freedom. One of my best friends, Christa was heading to KU in Lawrence (where a lot of our friends ended up), so I decided to tag along. We moved into an apartment with our friends Lisa (convulsion co-conspirator), Amy, and another girl I didn't know and can't remember her name. Our other friend Sheri lived close and joined in on the crazy often. We had some really great times in that apartment, but at the end of the semester, Christa and I decided we missed our boyfriends (I can't believe we were such wimps!) and headed back to Wichita. Unfortunately, between the upheaval, emotions, and physiology wired for anything other than school, I wasn't really racking up the credit hours. The mandatory classes killed me. I was more excited to explore classes such as the infamous "underwater basket-weaving." English and math? Come on! I've taken those for twelve years! Give me some spice! After being in college for a year and ending up back home in Wichita, I took a semester off to regroup. Not knowing which direction I was heading, I was truly hoping to find my "spice" when I went back to WSU the following semester.

There is this internal thing I have that's kind of like a moral compass. When I don't feel like I'm giving my best or doing a good job, an uncomfortable vibration radiates throughout my body. It's very stressful to feel that vibration, so I stay on *this* side of evil to keep it at bay. I think that this compass plays a big role in my perfectionism. I do things perfectly, because if I give less than perfect, a silent alarm goes off. This alarm was blaring through my body due to my less than decent attempts to succeed in classes that I didn't enjoy. If that wasn't enough to change my course, the thought of letting my parents down was. I knew even then how incredibly lucky I was that my mom was paying for my college. To be honest, if I would have had to pay for the torture of school myself, I can't promise that I would have stayed. For that reason alone, I'm thankful that she gave me the opportunity. I decided once again to start a self-improvement plan, so I could turn the "I'm a loser" siren off. I decided to commit to finishing my degree at WSU. That was huge, as I still, to this day, have a real problem committing to things or people.

After deciding to stick with WSU, I needed to see exactly which direction I wanted to go in for a career. My whole life I had pictured myself on TV or in the movies, and nothing else ever occurred to me. I used to get out my mom's video camera (it was huge and recorded to VHS tapes) and do newscasts, commercials, and short films (the editing was done by pushing the record button on and off). Nobody was safe from appearing in my productions. I used MTV VJs and correspondents as a study tool, because I could never relate to the anchors on the network news teams with their tidy suits and short-coiffed hair. I felt constricted just watching them. Broadcast journalism was definitely an avenue I could pursue, but I also felt an affinity for marketing and advertising. It was extremely confusing, and I needed to make the right choice, because I was going to commit to my decision, and once I make a commitment, I don't back down. Remember, I'm an all-or-nothing kind of girl.

While checking out programs involved with the different majors, I was invited by the journalism teacher (who gives me advice to this day, thanks to Facebook…hi, Jesse!) to check out his project, Studio B, which was a live newscast that was written, directed, produced, shot, and anchored by students. I have to say, I fell in love the minute they counted down to the opening of that first newscast I witnessed. I was so mesmerized by everything that took place; I was floating by the time it was over. I left that day knowing exactly which direction I was supposed to take and immediately made an appointment with an advisor. The alarm was no longer going off, and I felt a freedom I hadn't experienced in a while. It's always good when your path is lit by blazing torches before you—when there is no doubt in your mind that your chosen direction is indeed the right way to go. I had quite a few general classes to get through before I could really get into the meat (or veggies in my case) of the Studio B experience, but I was ready to face those challenges. There was no better motivator for me in college than Studio B.

After meeting with the advisor, I was slightly deflated to find out exactly how long it would take to get through my general classes. There were some prerequisites to Studio B that I needed to take before I could really participate.

Suddenly, the little hamster wheel in my brain began to creak as it started spinning. I knew I could take an active role in speeding up the process if I put my mind to it (hello, instant gratification!). I was also afraid that if I didn't get through school fast enough, I might not ever make it because of burn out. With a new spark, I sat down, and planned out every single class I needed to graduate with a BA in broadcast journalism. It took me two days to complete my geeky chart, but I finally got it all worked out, and that chart was a beauty. There was only one minor problem. On my chart, my goal was to graduate in two years. It was going to be hard, but not impossible. If I took twenty-four credit hours each fall and spring and eighteen credit hours each summer, I could do it. Because that kind of class load is technically insane, I had to get special permission from a guidance counselor to make myself crazier than I already was. Permission for crazy was granted, and I was able to plow through that semester and knock off enough prerequisites and general classes that I could enroll in Studio B the following semester. I was really proud of myself at the end of that semester. It *was* totally insane keeping up with all of those classes, but I pulled it off with a B-/C+ average. Seems like low grades for a perfectionist, huh? I guess I was just proud of myself for giving my all. I never really learned proper study skills in school, and always procrastinated, waiting to study and write papers the night before, when I would then pull all-nighters (that's assuming I remembered about the test or paper in the first place). Ahh…I loved those all-nighters. Christa and I would go to a coffee shop and hang out, studying and drinking coffee. It was so peaceful in the middle of the night; it allowed me to relax and get a lot accomplished.

So my weird study skills didn't allow me to achieve my best in grades, but it was the only way I knew how to motivate myself—by making seemingly impossible things possible. Remember? "It's either hot or cold, there's no lukewarm for me." My mom used to try to fix that for me. In her eyes, I was procrastinating and then scrambling to get it finished by the deadline. In reality, with my lack of executive function skills, it is physiologically impossible for me to meet any sort of deadline unless I have intense pressure motivating me. Where she sees the stress as a negative result of procrastination, I see the stress as my only motivator. The stress is the only thing that actually allows me to complete projects. Without the stress, I have no other skills to adjust for my lack of executive function skills. Without stress and pressure, it's a free-for-all in this brain. "Oh…just do it tomorrow…you need to relax. It'll still be there tomorrow"…on and on, until three years later nothing is accomplished. So, please people, if you know someone with AD(H)D, don't try to change that about them. Don't take that one skill away, or make them feel ashamed to use it. Sometimes procrastination is all they have in their little superhero tool belt!

Finally, the next semester arrived and I was in Studio B. I changed my on-air name to "McKinley" for about two weeks, until I finally started getting annoyed that people were actually calling me "McKinley." *That's not my damned name…Stop calling me that…I'm going back to Stacey!* I was able to completely lose myself in that class, and would gladly spend twenty to thirty hours a week working on my assignments. We would be assigned stories, and go out and collect footage and interviews to make our news stories. I was also the interviewer during the live newscast, so I interviewed a different guest every week. My first guest was Thunder Dog, the mascot for the Wichita hockey team. Whose idea was that? Do mascots even speak? What kind of questions did I ask him? I wish I could remember! I made some special friends in Studio B, a lot of whom I'm still in touch with. I became really close to a guy named Svein, and whenever I could, I would take him out with me as my videographer. We would wrap up our shooting, and then edit for hours and hours together. He always had amazing ideas, and we often had really out-of-the-box stories and video put together. He liked my "renegade anchor" style and I liked that there was nothing that man couldn't do. Svein and I actually won the best "News Package" in the state of Kansas for the KAB (Kansas Association of Broadcasters) Student Broadcast Awards. It was one of the proudest moments of my life. As the "anti-anchor" anchor and reporter, I was the underdog. We did a really cool MTV-style story about the Student Body President elections. We had video of the loser bawling his eyes out after he lost (which I must admit, I got a sick kind of kick out of, as I had "history" with this particular blubbering fellow). This was not your typical, conservative news story, but we were recognized as the best from student broadcasters all over Kansas. I was over the moon that night—those silly awards seem to give me such a sense of accomplishment. I am thankful for those times, because I wouldn't have grown as much professionally or creatively without Svein guiding me along. He was so incredibly gifted and is still to this day one of the most multitalented people I know. He's now a videographer for Fox National News.

Studio B

An interview with Thunder Dog. How awkward does that look? Were we just sitting there staring at each other for three minutes? I wish I could remember!

As a big project for one of our classes taught by our favorite hippie teacher, Rick; Svein and I wrote, directed, produced, and hosted our own magazine show called *Pastiche*. There were segment producers that did their own stories, and we put everything together. It was my first taste of hosting something other than a newscast. I loved the creative freedom; I loved finding a way to fit it all together holistically and feeling so passionate about what we were presenting. (We were friends with all of the segment producers and felt connected to their stories.) I got an almost addictive sense of accomplishment when that show was over. I really started to believe what my parents had always told me. *Was it true? I can do anything I set my mind to? Hmm.* I got a taste of something I liked, which gave me something to work for as my sense of direction was starting to waver. By the time I was nearing graduation and after multiple internships, I was absolutely positive that I did not want to have anything to do with broadcast news. I was not even semi-interested in being a news anchor at that point. The empathic part of me found it nearly impossible to work around the negativity reported in 98 percent of the news, let alone to write stories on it, or later, as an anchor, deliver it like Rosemary's baby to homes across the city. No thanks! For my final internship, I ended up in the sports department at a local station, and I sucked. My heart wasn't in it, and with me that's a death sentence.

I had two goals at that point; (1) to be the host of my own TV show or (2) to be a cast member on *Saturday Night Live*. I learned about my penchant for physical comedy as a guest in a Mormon Church talent show. How many people can say that? Before I was religiously bullied by Christians, I would often go to church with my friend, who happened to be a Mormon. Having lived in Utah for three years, the idea wasn't foreign to me at all. One night the church had a huge party for all of its members, and every youth class was to perform a skit on their huge stage. For ours, we had an "exercise class," but each person was actually made up of two people. One person laid flat with their legs out straight. The other person straddled their stomach with their legs tucked back. Throw a towel on to cover up the knees and it looked like one person. There was an exercise instructor, and we were all supposed to follow her lead. The bottom couldn't see what the hell was going on, so legs were all over the place. I was the top, so I was able to use my upper body, arms and facial expressions, and after a few encouraging laughs from the audience, I went NUTS hamming it up. I was making old ladies cry from laughing so hard. There is no other feeling like making an old lady cry. I was in complete flow on that stage. I was in another reality. I was in the most perfect state of balance, and I'm afraid, after twenty-seven years since my debut, I'll never feel that way again. OK, so hosting my own show or appearing on *Saturday Night Live* were pretty lofty goals, but back then it never occurred to me that I wouldn't achieve one or the other. I absolutely, positively knew that one of those jobs would come into my life.

Remember the math deficit I have faced my entire life? Well, don't think that went anywhere. I was finally in my last semester of college (yes, I actually did stick with that grueling schedule I had masochistically set up for myself, which resulted in giving me the confidence I needed to join the humans in the work force. See how that all magically works out?), and I had made it through every class, except one…algebra. I had already failed five times, which meant my mom had paid for it five times. I couldn't even think about algebra without breaking into a sweat. It was the only class left for me to take before I was able to graduate from college. I finally called a meeting with the advisor, and slightly broke down about my situation. She felt sorry for me and said I needed to meet with a psychologist on campus who could do an evaluation. My ears perked at that. There *is* a way to get out of algebra, and they said it couldn't be done! Mwahaha! I was with the psychologist for ten minutes (nine of those included heavy, dramatic sobbing on my part) before she declared an algebraic mental block and sent me back to the advisor with a note. The advisor read the note, walked out of the office, and returned ten minutes later. She smiled and told me that due to my mental block, I was hereby released from the tortures of algebra and would be able to take a different class of her choice in its place. I readily agreed—I'd take upside-down butt-hair clipping if I needed it to graduate. Funny thing is, the class she chose for me to take was parenting, and to this day I sincerely regret that I didn't pay better attention in that class. I somehow missed the "Secrets to Sane Parenting" chapter, but I digress; my plethora of parenting horror stories is for another book entirely.

Section Three:
Workin' It

"Not all who wander are lost."

—J. R. R. Tolkien

Chapter 8

I looked at that furry face, said, "Touché, baby monkey... touché," and walked away with whatever dignity I had left.

After graduation, it didn't take me long to land my first real job. It was one of those "it's who you know" things. One of my best friends from college, Brett, had graduated the year before me, and was holding down a promotions and marketing assistant position at the local FOX affiliate station. He was going in the direction of sales, and the position would soon be vacant. I sent in my résumé and was called for an interview. After writing some sample promo scripts for *The Simpsons* and *Married with Children*, I survived two more interviews before I was finally hired. I'm pretty sure it was my script for a *Star Trek* promo that won the heart of my soon-to-be boss, Tom. He was a total Trekkie, and I dug that about him. I love to see passion, in any form. A passionate person is alive, and if you're lucky, some of their passion may rub off on you...unless you don't like Star Trek, of course...then that would kind of suck.

That whole *winning his heart* thing? Turns out I was wrong. On my first day of work at KSAS, Tom didn't really speak to me. I thought it was a bit weird, but assumed he was just really busy. I began to suspect something was fishy when one week, two weeks, three weeks had gone by, and he still hadn't really spoken to me. I was positive he hated my guts. When I went into his office to ask questions, I could tell I made him really uncomfortable. I had to ask around to try to figure out what I was supposed to be doing for my job. About a month into it, Tom started coming around. And by *coming around* I mean actually speaking to me without my starting the conversation. I guess he was finally relaxing around me. For some reason, I always assume that people immediately don't like me when we meet, which is where I think I developed my taste for self-deprecation. Looking back, I can see that he was a very calm, soft-spoken guy that detests confrontation, and I'm best described as the opposite.

As the promotions and marketing assistant, it was my job to come up with promotional ideas and help carry them out. Well, that was part of my job. The other part was acting as the runner. Every day after lunch, I would hop in the horrendous KSAS station wagon to deliver and/or pick up scripts, tapes, giant chocolate bunnies, or whatever, from the local TV and radio stations as well as ad agencies. I would look at the in-box with all of my errands, and then plan the route accordingly. I slowly came to detest that part of the job. Every day I had to drive on the same boring streets, go to the same boring places, and talk to the same boring people about the same boring things. Every. Day. I started resenting those little white sheets in my in-box, and for me, resentment is the kiss of death. When I resent something, I spend an enormous amount of energy trying to psyche myself up to be able to deal with it, which makes me hate it even more. I can literally make myself sick about it. Luckily for me, there was something on the horizon that would break me out of the runner's madness that was slowly overtaking my work life.

One day I was called into Tom's office. As I skipped in (you can probably understand why Tom had a slight aversion to me), I noticed the program director sitting on one of the chairs across from Tom's desk. I thought, "Oh shit. What did I do now?" Was I still getting in trouble for things, you ask? Of course I was—for totaling the station's SUV (not my fault), getting something in my eye that required me leaving work and going to the doctor (again, not my fault, and who knew you could get written up for getting hurt?), getting too many phone calls (not my fault; I wasn't the one calling), getting back late for lunch (OK, I'll take the blame for that one), and so on. To be fair, the office manager really had it out for me. She did not like young, fun girls at all. I'm pretty sure she even hated animals. I laugh now, as I wonder why I was never caught doing the truly naughty things like falling asleep at my desk every day (probably due to my excessive partying every night... except Sundays...for some reason, we took Sunday night off), or smoking clove cigarettes in the station wagon while making my runs, or editing promos while I was high. I actually only did that once. It wasn't a very good experience. Well, it was, and it wasn't. My friend Brett (the one who got me the job, ironically) walked into the editing suite to find me half-hanging out of my chair, tears swimming down my red face, choking with laughter from trying to edit a *Simpsons* promo. I could not even function, I was laughing so hard. He had to close the door and try to calm me down before someone came in to see what all of the ruckus was about. Every now and then I'll watch *The Simpsons* just to try to catch a little piece of the magic from that day in the editing suite.

As you can imagine, there was a plethora of reasons why I would be called in there and I hadn't the foggiest idea which one I was getting busted for. I just braced myself. To my immense relief, it ended up that they *hadn't* found out that I was using the storage loft in the studio for naptime (when I got tired of sleeping upright at my desk). It turns out that they were starting production on a local TV show, and *they needed a freaking host*! By that time, I had done endless commercials, and they knew I could at least memorize. They explained the concept of the show, and asked if I would be interested in being the host. Would I? Would I! Do cats carry the odor around for a full five minutes after taking a poop? Yes! I was ready to rock and roll. I was born to do this. I knew this was the beginning of something special. I knew then, for sure, that I absolutely could do anything I set my mind to. Anything. This was the result of my manifestation, and I had been preparing for this my entire life. It sounds dramatic, but it *was* dramatic! To realize how much power I had in directing my own life gave me an enormous amount of confidence.

The show was called *Flash TV.* We had "Flash Cards" distributed throughout the public school system in Wichita. Those cards held discounts for local restaurants, movies, music, games, sports, and so on. I once heard a rumor that the sponsors paid twenty-five-thousand-dollars per year to be on our card, except for Pizza Hut, who paid more and was our major sponsor. The salespeople had to go out and sell the concept to their accounts. They actually got quite a few sponsors, which was great, except at some point those salespeople needed to kiss ass and occasionally had us incorporate their clients into segments on the show, like the day I hosted from *Subway* as a "sandwich artist."

Our *Flash TV* family consisted of myself, Chris, John, Ken, Scott, and Phyllis. The guys were the production team, and Phyllis was the art director at the station. We still had to carry on with our regular responsibilities and fit *Flash TV* into our normal schedule. Because the concept of this show was a mere shell, we had to fill in the pieces and make things up as we went along. We worked a lot of extra hours and spent a lot of extra time together, but it was one of the most in-flow times of my life…emotionally, creatively, professionally, and any other "ly" word that fits. Though I would get letters on occasion from fans that really liked what we were doing, I mostly got letters from prisoners that were locked-up tight, only about an hour way from the station. You'd think prisoners would be fans of a young, decent-looking girl having adventures for their viewing pleasure, but that wasn't the case. They hated my show, they hated me, and they loved to tell me about it—a paragraph from each of the prisoners, consolidated into one long letter of disgust after each episode. It was awesome, and I still have one of the letters to this day. I always wondered why they didn't just change the channel in the prison commons, but I enjoyed the letters too much to protest. You'd think I'd be offended, but I guess I'd rather have them hate me than to feel indifferent toward me. At least I was invoking some kind of passion! Needless to say, we did have a few requests for autographed photos, so we had to come up with an 8x10 glossy to mail out with my signature. Unfortunately for our fans, who were few and far between, the *glossy* magically morphed into *photocopy* when our budget didn't allow for the glossy part. That's right—every fan that requested an autographed picture received a photocopy of an autographed picture. I don't even have the glossy! The only copy in my box of *FLASH TV* memorabilia was delivered to me as a fourth-generation Xerox.

Flash Television - prisoners hate it

The autographed photo. Enough said.

Interviewing Goo Goo Dolls. Still love them!

Every segment of every show was always an adventure. Those pesky sales-people trying to kiss the ass of their clients led to a few of those adventures. Dave, the biggest ass kissing offender, had a client that owned a seedy, dirty, resale appliance shop in the bad part of town. I guess this guy had some land with cattle and horses, and Dave wanted us to do a segment where I learned to rope and ride. We showed up with the cameras and met Dave and the client on his land. With a fake goat or sheep or whatever it was, he taught me to rope, first on the ground and then from a horse. I'm a big fan of animals, so I was, much to my dismay and Dave's delight, having a great time with his questionable client. During my riding lesson (and taping of the show), my majestic horse started farting and continued to do so for a good five minutes straight, while we trotted. I was laughing too hard to even question if stopping the horse would stop the gas. My stomach was so weak from laughing, I couldn't hold my body up, so I was flopping all around on top of this horse as he was stink-bombing the place. It was a sight to see, but I didn't even care how uncool I looked—I was just trying to hold on at that point.

I really can't make fun of the horse, though, because I had my own ass-capade in front of the camera. Well, at least behind the microphone. We were out shooting the opening to a segment, and for some reason, we had two cameras going. I'm not sure how to say this delicately, so I'll just say it. I was having a hemorrhoid issue. Actually, there were multiple hemorrhoids. I still have no idea what I did to inflict so much butt pain on myself. The hemorrhoids were so painful, I went to the doctor. He told me to get some Tucks pads and prescribed some pain pills. Less educated about chemicals back then, I took them while I was working. Doped up, I definitely felt less pain, but that also meant that I didn't realize that the Tucks pad, that I had inserted like a taco between my butt cheeks, had spread a massive wet stain on my jeans, not to mention that you could clearly see the outline of the pad, as it had escaped its enclosure and created a circle that spread across both cheeks. As I said, our team was really close, and I liked to share my daily adventures so they all knew about my problem. They also thought it would be funny to keep me out of the loop about what was going on behind me in my jeans. At that point, I had another issue. I was starting to feel really nauseous from the pain pills.

I finally went into the bathroom for the inevitable. I started throwing up, and continued to do so for ten minutes. After the first three pukes, it was nothing but dry heaves. We all know what dry heaves sound like, right? Not attractive. Especially when there's some unintelligible gibberish thrown in after each heave! Well, much to my dismay and delight, I had been wearing a wireless microphone, so during my entire ordeal in the bathroom, the guys had been taking turns with the headphones listening to me yack. They didn't want me to miss out on the fun, so they recorded it. I didn't find out until later that day at the station. I had finally regained my composure and was busy working when I turned a corner and saw a bunch of people gathered around one of our tape players. All of the production guys were there, along with some sales guys, and maybe even a few guys from engineering! I wouldn't have thought much about it, but when they saw me come around that corner, their eyes got wide, their faces paled, and I swear to God they, each and every one, nearly pooped their grown-man pants. Ah ha! My eyes narrowed, and a growl escaped from the back of my throat. As a twenty-one-year-old girl working primarily with men, I had to be tough. I had to learn to take a lot of shit, and, more importantly, to give that shit back. I'm pretty sure I looked mad, and they had seen me lose my temper countless times, but apparently that wasn't enough to stop the snorting that quickly escalated in intensity due to the effort of holding back their laughter. I looked at the group and demanded an explanation. Scott called me over to the player, and everyone made some room so I could listen to the guttural, wild animal noises coming out of the speakers. It wasn't until I recognized the saliva-drenched gibberish that I realized those noises had been coming from me as I puked uncontrollably earlier that day (all the while with a Tucks stain on my butt, which I didn't become aware of until they showed me the video we had shot). Those guys! I have to admit, the whole thing was wickedly funny, and I even played that puke audio again for anyone that missed it the first time.

As you can probably tell, I seem to get into a lot of predicaments. I used to think the universe had something against me, but my friend McLovin explained to me that I put myself out there more so than the average person, and the seemingly excessive predicaments were just a result of basic statistics. What a simple explanation. It's not bad Karma—it's math!

One afternoon we headed over to the Sedgwick County Zoo to do a segment on the new Orangutan exhibit that had just opened. We were assigned a host from the zoo that walked around with us, giving us access to nonpublic areas so we could get the best shots of the Orangutans. At one point we were up against the bars feeding them and giving them juice boxes to drink. They were so close I could touch them. It was amazing. It was such a good spot visually; I decided to do my stand-up there. I had turned my back to the bars and was facing the camera, doing my bit, when I felt something grab my hair on the left side of my head and pull me back into the bars. I instantly thought of the show *When Animals Attack*, which had just aired on our station. I hadn't even completed the thought when I felt fingers hook into the right side of my mouth from behind. Something was giving me the fishhook! I couldn't move as my head was pinned back. In a flurry of activity, the poor zoo guy was at my side trying to disengage my hair and my mouth from the furry, orange fingers! As he freed first my mouth and then my hair, I spun around to confront my attacker. I found myself looking into the mischievous eyes of a baby orangutan hanging on to the cage, right in front of me. He looked like a stuffed animal and was probably about the size of a two-year-old. That little bastard had LMFAO written all over its face. I challenge anyone to look at the footage and deny that he wore the epitome of the expression "shit-eating grin." I couldn't believe how obvious the satisfaction was! After a brief stare-down, I shrugged my shoulders and finally acknowledged that I've worn that same expression countless times, and this most likely *was* a case of Karma. Happy that I wasn't mauled, and we had caught it for our outtakes, I looked at that furry face, said, "Touché, baby monkey…touché" and walked away with whatever dignity I had left. I know, I know, Orangutans aren't monkeys. I guess I had other things on my mind…like coming *this* close to getting my lips and eyebrows ripped off.

Flash TV was going great. I was soaking up tons of information as I was exposed to every facet of producing a TV show, and it kept my brain constantly stimulated. There wasn't a day I can think of that I wasn't excited to go into work. Part of my promotions job called for me to work with the art/graphics department. I would go to them when I needed art designed for my promotions. As I watched my ideas manifest before my eyes, I became fascinated with graphic design. When I could, I would sit beside the designers, watching every click as they brought the screen to life with their creations. I began to stay after work sitting in front of the graphics computer, puttering around in the software. I became very adept at getting around, and I began doing some of my own graphic design. It was good for me, because I was learning something new. It was good for Phyllis and the art department, because it freed up some of their time for everything else they had going on. Not only were they overscheduled, the assistant art director, Lesley, was kind of a flake, and began acquiring quite a few absences. At that point, people at the station knew I was capable (and for a self-learner, quite good) as a graphic designer, and began bringing the assignments to me if Lesley wasn't available. Things began to get really hectic for me as I was doing my promotions job, hosting and co-producing *Flash TV*, and now tackling bits of design work. I'm not whining, because as I said before, I really enjoyed every aspect of my job, except for the runner part, but the clove cigarettes lessened the monotony of that bit. I just didn't have enough time in the day. My cat naps were a thing of the past. Pretty soon I started hearing whispers of Lesley getting tossed. I liked the lady, but she was completely unreliable, and I was sick of doing her job for none of her pay. I just hoped whomever they hired would let me tinker around on their stuff.

Over a month had passed since Lesley was asked to hit the road, and we still didn't have an assistant art director. I was crazy busy, but I was in heaven. On top of my other responsibilities, I was now sitting in as the assistant art director. Finally, it got to a point where it was physically impossible to do all three jobs. Again I was called into Tom's office, and again I probably skipped on in there, but by then he was used to my shenanigans. Phyllis was in there, which meant I probably wasn't in trouble, since we were really tight. They both wore goofy smiles. I don't remember the details, but they basically asked me if I wanted to give up the promotions job and become the official assistant art director. I was shocked. They wanted me to be a graphic designer. I didn't know how to be a graphic designer! I thought they were insane for even suggesting it, and I told them so! They assured me that that were indeed sane, and that I was perfectly capable of doing the job. It's the first time I remember having the feeling that I was tricking everyone around me. Do you ever feel that way? Like you're just tricking people, and you aren't who they think you are, and you can't do what they think you can, and when you do, it's just dumb luck, and it wouldn't happen twice? I read somewhere that they did a poll of Mensa members, and something like 85 percent of them believed that if they had to take the Mensa entrance exam again, they wouldn't pass it. They actually believed they only passed the first time with sheer dumb luck. I find that fascinating and remind myself of it often, especially when I'm feeling less than confident.

Because the unknown is constantly trying to seduce me, I agreed to become the assistant art director. Tom was still my main boss, but I reported to Phyllis. No more runs! I had a blast doing that job. I realize now why I was so successful, as far as being happy goes, and it boils down to two things. I didn't have any long-term projects. I had small projects that I could usually complete in one, two, or three hours. That allowed me to cross four, five, or sometimes more things off my list per day, and I could see my accomplishments. The second was that I was constantly learning and being challenged, so it kept me stimulated. There was structure, which I need immensely, but also the freedom within that structure to do things my way. At the end of the day when I was straightening my desk (just kidding...I always left it in total disarray, which is something else I always got in trouble for), I felt such an overwhelming sense of accomplishment that my brain, both the right and the left sides, would just purr.

One of the sales guys, Phil, was an avid skydiver. I went skydiving with him for a segment on *Flash TV*. Looking back, that guy had AD(H)D written all over his forehead. He loved the thrill of jumping from planes, he really dug sales (I'm an introvert, so sales is not my gig, but lots of AD[H]Ders love sales), and he was an idea man. He decided that the world needed skydiving ties, so he figured out where to find the silky skydiver fabric, figured out who would make them, and then proceeded to start production, all while doing his sales job at the station. It didn't take long before the grumblings started. People thought he was spending his day selling the neckties instead of advertising. I knew he was, because he had already asked me to do some art projects for him on the side.

One day Phil came to my desk, and started to hem and haw, making small talk. I knew he was going to ask me something, and I just wanted him to get it over with. He could be slightly overbearing some times, kind of like a hyper kid, and I had crap to do. He finally told me that he had put in his notice. He was going to start his own advertising agency, and he wanted me to be the art director. He had a couple of big clients that had already signed on, and he was confident that he could acquire more clients shortly.

I told him that I wanted to think about it, and I did so that night. I had really come to love graphic design. I never felt more productive than when I was designing, and feeling productive is as necessary as water to me. Changing jobs would mean more money, more responsibility, and change. I was really going to miss my friends at the station, and I knew it would mean giving up the show, but I have a fear of stagnation, and I liked the idea of leaving my job while I still enjoyed it, instead of waiting for it to get monotonous. I really think that's why I have such fond memories of that place and time in my life.

Chapter 9

If patience is a virtue, then I'm a filthy whore, because once I get going on something, it takes a Jedi Knight to stop me in my tracks.

I accepted the position. Or, rather, what I thought was the position. I started a month later. Phil had also recruited one of his skydiving buddies, Kent, as a salesman. In the beginning we all shared an office in Phil's basement. I think we were there six weeks or so before Phil found a real office for us. Funny thing is, in that short, six-week span of time, I went from being a designer of advertising to designing skydiving apparel. How the hell did that happen, you ask? Well Phil decided that on top of the new ad agency he had just started, it would be fun to expand his skydiving brand from ties to a whole catalog's worth of clothes, and I was in charge of the design of the shirts, catalog, advertising, and so on. In other words, in the midst of starting his new business, he began another new business: custom and mail-order skydiving clothes. I know; I was as confused as you are.

The new office reflected our need for warehouse space, as we were going to be responsible for taking, filling, and shipping the orders, on top of our own jobs. We were getting the t-shirts screen printed, and then Phil figured out if he ordered the shirts and gave those to the printer instead of using the printer's stock, he could save money. After doing that for a while, he decided that we would save even *more* money if we bought our *own* printing press, and hired a screen printer to print them in the warehouse at the office. That was fine for a bit until he decided that we should not only print *our* shirts, but charge others to print *their* shirts. That's right! We are now an advertising agency/sky diving apparel company/screen printer. Even that wasn't enough, because then Phil decided that to be a screen printer we needed to have a real shop. He negotiated with our original printer, bought his screen printing shop, and kept him on to run it. Things got ugly fast. Phil was starting to run out of money, so we had to say good-bye to the office and relocate to the shop. I was now also designing for the regular screen printing customers that had been going to the original shop for years. The environment was pissy, chaotic, loud, stinky, and stressful. I was in the only office, but had a reaction to the mold that was growing in the corner, so I was moved to the front entrance. I'm serious. You walk in the door and BAM, there I was. It had been a year, and I was miserable. I need a stable environment, and I need consistency, neither of which had been available to me for the past twelve months. I had given it a good shot, but it was time to get out before I shriveled away from misery and my lungs sprouted fields of mold spores.

As I was desperate to get out, I took the first opportunity presented to me, which was radio sales. It ended up being horrible for me. It was so horrible that I quit before I had secured another job. There is no better feeling than launching an entire burden from your shoulders in one heave. I quit. Immediate peace. There is no fear of the unknown, no questioning the future. Everything *has* to turn out OK, because that decision felt so *right*. On paper it was stupid, but I tend to go with how I feel, and it felt really good. I understand that some people aren't as connected to their intuition as I am, so when a person is coming strictly from a logical standpoint, sometimes my choices may seem a little out there. I get it—I don't care, but I do get it.

With an extra bounce in my step, I walked into a temp agency the next morning. The manager and I both lived in lofts that sat above the agency, and we had become good friends. After a couple hours of testing, I was presented with a job opportunity. It was a good match for my background, yet something I hadn't considered before: market research. They needed a marketing associate. Unfortunately for me, the job description included answering the phone. I detest answering phones, especially multi-line phones. It's a multi-tasking thing that always ends up with someone forgotten on hold or hung up on. Plus, it always pisses me off when I'm in the middle of something and I have to stop and answer the phone. I just want to scream into the receiver, "Don't you people know I have a hard time with transitions!" That could portray me as unstable, so forgetting that I was in Wichita, Kansas, I dismissed it and asked what other jobs were available that didn't require answering a phone. After shuffling through some papers, the HR director said, "It looks like they're all clerical jobs that require you to answer the phone." I felt my shoulders slump as my professional gift to the world was reduced to being filed in the clerical category. None of the other positions were in the marketing or advertising field, so I went back to the original offer and accepted it.

It didn't pay as well, but it had its perks. It was located downtown, within walking distance of my apartment, and the word "marketing" appeared somewhere in the job title. I was introduced to reality when, within five minutes of clocking in on my first day, I was told by the office manager, Barb, that I would share equally in the office chores, which included cleaning the toilets. I'm so thankful that I was born without the ability to regret, because I would have been kicking my own ass, right then, for ever leaving KSAS and *Flash TV* to end up cleaning toilets and answering phones. I'm not saying there's anything wrong with having a job that requires either one, I'm just saying, I wouldn't have been the best candidate, as I can't even keep my own damned toilets clean *nor* answer my own freaking phone. Fortunately, I'm able to see most things as an adventure, and nervously laughed as I agreed to partake in equal toilet duty.

Two colleagues in the marketing department at Wichita State owned the company. Unfortunately, I had taken a marketing class from one of the owners, Bob, that ended with a "D" on my record, and to my horror, he later admitted that he had looked up my grades after I was hired when he found out I was WSU alum. Poor guy. After looking at that, he must have not expected much from me in the area of employment! Sometimes that isn't a bad thing, though. Isn't it better when people are pleasantly surprised rather than mildly disappointed by that which is you? I could waste time being offended that their expectations of me are low to begin with, but it's much more rewarding to use that energy to knock their fucking socks off by my genius! *Genius* might be a little overdramatic, but you catch my drift.

I proceeded to win over the hearts of the powers-that-be and a couple months later, when they were *really* serious, they bought me out of my contract with the temp agency, and gave me a raise. I ended up really loving my job, my bosses, and everyone that worked there. We were like a family, so sometimes there were disagreements, but I was given that flying room I so desperately need. I was allowed to tackle anything I fancied! Though I did have to answer the phone, since it was a small office I got to put my hands in everything, which I have found to be key in keeping me interested in any job. Throughout my three or so years there, I did everything from making signs for the bathroom (some poem about what not to flush down the loo) to moderating diaper studies. I don't recall ever having to actually clean the toilets. Does poop and pee seem to be the reoccurring theme here? That's not even intentional; I swear. As I said, we were like a family, and occasionally I would get in trouble for one thing or another. I would say what tops the list is the time I had to present market research results to a bank president with unintentional purple hair. Bob and the other owner, Esther, soon learned that with my nonlinear brain I was able to look over research and then provide a solid picture of what that the research was showing, so sometimes they would take me along on meetings to answer a client's very specific questions.

One night I impulsively decided to color my hair "plum." Though impulsively deciding to cut or color my hair was nothing new, I had never gone that specific shade before. Unfortunately, it wasn't complimentary to my skin tone, as it was more purple than plum. Since impulsivity requires absolutely no forethought whatsoever, I never said to myself, *Gee, Stace...are you sure you want to try out a new color, specifically one called "plum," that could turn out iffy, the night before an important meeting? Maybe you should wait until tomorrow night, en caso que.* If patience is a virtue, then I'm a filthy whore, because once I get going on something, it takes a Jedi Knight to stop me in my tracks.

The next day, I wore a bandana to work to make the purple hair less obvious and immediately received a snort from Bob and the stink-eye from Esther. Great. I needed to take care of the stink-eye first. I went to Esther's office and explained the purpose of the apparently offensive head accessory. When I showed her my purple hair, she transitioned from stink-eye to eye-roll, and made me call my hairstylist on the spot. Thank God Patty was accustomed to fixing my "creativity." Unfortunately, she had no time available in the following hour, so I still had to go to the bank meeting that morning donning the bandana (it was a toss-up on which was more hideous). Esther started the meeting off by apologizing for my unsightly and completely offensive appearance. Bob was Bob and just thought the whole thing was funny. He always got a kick out of my pickles. Work only became more enjoyable after my crazy friend, Carrie, started, so I stayed on until I moved to my next destination: sunny San Diego.

I had some interviews set up before I moved and secured a job two weeks after arriving. I was excited because it was in advertising, and paid the highest salary I had commanded to date. I was an account executive, so I would be responsible for servicing any advertising accounts assigned to me. There was one in particular that was a million dollar account seemingly starved for attention at all times, so, lucky me, that was going to be my primary account. Unfortunately, I was doomed before I even started, which was a change for me, because normally I'm entirely responsible for any doom occurring in my life. I'm usually happy to take blame, I really am, but not this time. Number one: the two clients I dealt with were serious dickheads. Number two: they had worshipped my predecessor, so I was what they considered the "inferior replacement." Only a few weeks after I started, they couldn't be bothered to continue hiding their distaste when I walked in the room. I'm pretty sure one of them even hissed at me during a TV spot approval meeting! My boss, Wayne, had to kiss their ass double-time just to stay at "barely getting the job done." I couldn't do anything right, even when I was actually doing something right. I'm not going to BS you, that was a really tough job for me, and I occasionally did things…ummm…wrong. There was just waaaaay too much shit for me to try to keep organized. Newspaper, TV, radio, direct mail, events, promotional items—they had a crap-load of locations in multiple states, with every location doing their own local advertising, and I was supposed to keep track of all that…with absolutely zero executive function skills whatsoever. That's like asking someone amputated at both shoulders to attempt juggling; it can happen, but it ain't gonna be pretty! I got sick of the craziness (mine and theirs) and ended up quitting almost a year later, after I was hired as an art director for a video-on-demand company. I knew it would be horrible by the end of the first day. My intuition doesn't fart around, and three days later by 10 a.m., it was screaming at me to walk out for lunch and never come back. Of course, I thought to myself that I couldn't actually do that, but it did give me a case of maniacal-sounding giggles to envision it. I'm not sure if there *is* an acceptable excuse for walking out on your job midday, but if so, I did not have it. I'm completely embarrassed to admit this, but the single most important reason I despised the job was because the owner walked around unabashedly with a hernia on his stomach that looked like one of the mushrooms from Super Mario was going to launch into space from his belly. It stuck out at least six inches, and was as big around as an IHOP pancake. You couldn't help but notice it every time he came into the room, and seeing it made my skin crawl. I don't know if it was because it looked like it might be painful, or if it just grossed me out. I'm weird like that. When I was in junior high, we would occasionally stop by McDonald's after school. They had an employee that was missing an arm and had a hook in its place. And not like a friendly hook….like a Captain Hook hook. Regardless, whenever I saw her, I would instantly lose my appetite. I could never figure out if I was grossed out or if I just felt bad that she was walking around with a fairy-tale weapon as an appendage. Anyway, same deal here. In the end, the issue was not where the feelings stemmed from, but how I was going to deal with them. I just couldn't handle having my skin crawl from eight to five, so that day I left for lunch and never returned. The maniacal giggles kicked in again as I drove home, not believing how out of my mind I was to have done what I just did. As I've said before, some of my decisions don't look good on paper, so I just go by how I feel, and a lot of people don't really understand that concept. Anyway, hysterical laughing aside, I felt good with the decision and have never regretted it.

Chapter 10

The most risqué thing I had done to Bob Dole was to shake my pregnant ass in the general direction of his crotch.…She was acting like I'd dry-humped his neck on stage.

Wayne forgave me for quitting and took me back the next week, only to fire me about three months later after hiring an office manager that came to the conclusion that my assistant could do my job better for less money. "It's not me, it's you." I actually blame Dave, for my getting fired. It was a Friday night, and as a team we went out to dinner to welcome the new office manager. We were riding back to the office to get our cars, and she, along with another person, happened to be riding with us. Dave was driving, and I'm not sure what happened, but for a split second he forgot we weren't alone, and proceeded to fart louder than anything I've ever heard in my life. A trumpet would have seemed like a whisper next to this fart. I have never been so mortified in my life, and I could tell by her face that the new lady was confused on whether to be scared or just plain pissed off. Needless to say, I lost my job the following Monday, and I'm pretty sure it was that enormous fart that got me fired.

My boss, Wayne, never really had good timing, and chose to fire me right before Dave and I left for our belated honeymoon in Maui. We had gotten married five months prior, in a wacky turn-of-events, but I'll tell you that story later. We switched our trip from Paris to Maui, because by the time it came to make the arrangements, we were in serious need of relaxation, and Paris sounded like the opposite of relaxing. A couple of weeks before we were scheduled to leave, Dave received an invitation to a basketball referee camp in L.A., which was apparently an honor, because Dave freaked out when he opened the envelope. When he showed me the invitation, I almost laughed out loud when I immediately realized it would be taking place while we were honeymooning. I know it says something about me that I thought that was funny, but he was just so excited, it made the whole situation funnier. I pointed the date out and cringed in expectation of his response. Awww...it was soooo sad...even more so than I thought it would be, and to my disappointment not in the least bit funny. I felt so terrible; I told him that he could leave our honeymoon two days early so he could make it to L.A. in time for his beloved camp. He wouldn't hear of it. Notice I said *he* could leave our honeymoon two days early. I wasn't planning on going anywhere! I finally twisted his arm (which took all of three minutes) and convinced him that he wasn't a terrible husband by going, so in the end, I stayed and spent the last two days of my honeymoon in Maui by myself. I enjoyed it almost equally without my husband around. I adore him beyond measure, but he does love to talk, and I'm a fan of peace and quiet.

Dave had just graduated, and I was out of a job. We saw a blank palette ahead of us, which was very exciting, because it meant we could paint our own canvas. Choose the brush...choose the colors...we were in charge. We had been having a lot of discussions about our future, and had come to the conclusion that San Diego was not the ideal place for us to live due to the horrendous cost of living. Since there were a lot of unknowns, we thought we would set up a temporary base camp somewhere while trying to figure our lives out. Kansas was the obvious choice, with it being inexpensive, closer to my parents in Texas, and filled with friends and family. We decided to move after the New Year, which was only three months away. Dave had some games to referee at the end of January, so the plan was for me to go early January, stay with Carrie, and find a job and an apartment before he arrived in early February.

By the time Dave and his dad rolled into Kansas with the U-Haul, I had a job with a nonprofit, and an apartment with a lease beginning the day before their scheduled arrival. The apartment was awesome. It was the same complex I had lived in before I moved to San Diego. The job, on the other hand, was not awesome. I'm not a huge fan of drama, and there was drama every single day at that place. My worst memory was when we hosted a roast of Bob Dole as a fundraiser. That day Patty, my trusty hairstylist, put long, blonde extensions in my hair, as I was going to perform that night as Britney Spears. Their Pepsi commercial together had recently come out, so we were spoofing it. The kicker was that, by that time, I was about five months pregnant with Willow, and it was obvious, so the joke was that Bob Dole had gotten me, "Britney," pregnant. You can imagine how nervous I was, as Bob had no idea this was going to happen to him on stage. At dinner before the show, I had a glass of wine to loosen up. The show went splendidly, and Bob got a kick out of the impersonation. According to my psychotic boss, the evening was a definite success.

Fast-forward to the next morning. I'm in her office and she tells me that my Bob Dole lap dance was too risqué, and that I had completely offended everyone around me for having a glass of wine with dinner, while pregnant. I felt like the lowest piece-of-shit-for-a-person on the earth. My blood boiled as she spoke. The most risqué thing I had done to Bob Dole was to shake my pregnant ass in the general direction of his crotch. She was acting like I'd dry-humped his neck on stage. Also, *she* was the person that offered me the wine in the first place, after exclaiming that I seemed nervous! Crazy was her MO, though. I replied back that I couldn't even believe she had the nerve to bring these things up to me. She later told me she couldn't believe how "bitchy and hormonal" I was during our discussion. She had no idea just how inappropriate she was. She constantly talked about sex, orgasms, and every other thing an unhappy wife has on their minds. It wasn't just sex talk; she was filthy-nasty, even on occasion talking about her panties getting wet. There was also a rumor that she was sleeping with one of *her* bosses. Anyway, by the time she was in my office, curled in the fetal position threatening suicide, I'd had about enough. We contacted HR about her state, and they opened an investigation, but nothing was ever done. I was seven months pregnant, and having to work in the postinvestigation chaos. My boss was still crazy, and now she also hated us with every crazy bone in her body. She was verbally, emotionally, and mentally abusive at all times. You could tell she was a ticking time bomb, and I didn't want to be around when she finally lost her mind, so I left…two and a half months away from giving birth. That environment had been so negative that I found it vital to focus on trying to relax and detox all of the stress hormones out of my body for my poor baby.

It's Britney Bitch.

Hey! Why is my hand in Bob Dole's shirt? That's me on Bob's right and my mom on his left. Everyone looks happy to me!

Not even a couple of weeks after I quit, Dave lost his job. I still didn't let myself stress out. I knew things were happening for a reason, and I was mostly excited to see what was in store for us. It wasn't hard to decide that the first change was going to be our location. With the baby's arrival looming, my intuition was pretty adamant that I was going to need to be near my own mom during this next adventure. I didn't know why, I just knew I would, and thank God I listened, because I ended up losing my mind after the baby came, and my new little family had a crazy mommy on their hands, and needed all of the extra emotional and physical support possible. I was *this* close to checking into a loony bin (being loony myself, I'm entitled to say *loony bin* without being offensive), but again, another book entirely!

We moved to Texas and lived with my mom and Bob when Willow was only two weeks old. We stayed there for six weeks before getting a loft apartment downtown, designed to make us feel as if we were still carefree. That was idea anyway. Dave's plan was to get into the teacher certification program. In the meantime, he secured a position as the counselor at a technical college. My friend Donya once again swooped in and bettered my life. Her friend Kerrie had a brother, Brad, that lived in the area and his collision shop was looking for a marketing director. After a few phone calls and an interview with Brad and the owner, I was offered the position. It wasn't a bad job. I had to call on car insurance offices to try to generate business for the body shop. It was all done with bribery such as cool little gifts and catered lunches. All of my potential clients were happy when I walked in the door every month, because they knew I was packing some goods. It made my job pretty easy to bear.

Not only was the job semi-fun, but I also loved the people I worked with. I became close with Brad and Kristi, the accountant. Pretty soon we were a threesome (not to be mistaken for *had* a threesome), even going out to party after our monthly meetings. It was all fun and games until the night I left them together drunk in his truck, in a restaurant parking lot. According to Kristi, not five minutes after they watched my taillights disappear, she had her panties off and our threesome was instantly downsized to a twosome. Nothing was ever the same after that. Brad wasn't interested in a relationship with Kristi, and Kristi had to pretend she wasn't falling in love with Brad. Of course, by continuing to have sex with her, Brad did nothing to convince her that she wasn't "the one." Though, you'd think she would know that by how often he actually told her he was not in love. He was a blunt man, to say the least. Bluntness did nothing to dissuade her, and she stupidly hung in there, crying in her office every day because of something Brad did or said to her. She cried about him, and he bitched about her. Naturally, I was always in the middle, a very annoying place indeed, but it wasn't until Kristi started accusing Brad and me of having our own affair, and treating me accordingly, that I had to throw in the towel. She had gone from friendly to certifiably nuts, and I couldn't hang out in that kind of wacky environment without becoming wackier myself. That's just my DNA, friend. I had to find a new job.

It know it sounds like I blame other people for my inability to stick with a job, but I actually don't. I take full responsibility for my reactions to their issues. I know there are certain things that really bother me that another person might not think twice about. But, since I was the lucky winner of this particular brain, for me, whatever the offense happens to be at any given time (tumors, hysteria, suicide attempts, whatever) causes enormous amounts of stress and anxiety, so my natural reaction is to just remove myself from the offending situation as soon as possible to minimize physical and emotional damage caused by the offense. It's called self-preservation, and I'm a *huge* fan. As I've said before, a lot of my personal energy and time is spent coping with what I have going on internally, so I don't have time to mess around with other people's crazy.

As luck would have it, there was an opening where my mom was employed. It was only part-time, but it was more money, so it evened out. The position was for an assistant to the president's administrative assistant. I was slightly worried about having an "assistant" job, because—let's be honest—an assistant needs to be organized, responsible, and pretty much every other weakness I employ, and the last place you want to parade your deficits around is in front of the president of a company. His assistant's name was Eva. My mom knew her and really liked her. She was well-respected, because she did *not* mess around. She kept a tight ship, and some people were even rumored to be afraid of her. Eva was the one that called me to set up an interview, and I met with her the following day. I'm not gonna lie…I was a little scared.

She was certainly intimidating by reputation, but I found her to put off a warm vibe in person and liked her immediately. After a nice tour and chat about the job, I was offered the position. I knew I would have some difficulties in a few areas, but I felt confident I could work through them, so I happily accepted. I have to admit, I was slightly freaked out when my first task was to wrap a gift for the wife of the soon-to-be president. It's not like it was a box, either. It was a funky shaped something-or-other. I was hired in the middle of a transition of presidents, so for the first six or so months of my job, Eva was supporting them both. Anyway, to me the "wrap a gift" thing was as equally distasteful as the "clean the toilet" thing. Actually, cleaning a toilet is probably more exciting…at least you're in "danger" of touching poop! Wrapping just sucks, and I suck at wrapping, though not as bad as I suck at getting Saran Wrap out of its container.

Eva already had one assistant. Her name was Linda, and she was artsy and awesome. Thankfully, she stepped in when she saw I was having a hard time making the bow on the gift look presentable. We got a good giggle out of my lack of skills and became fast friends. A few months into loving my job, my mom was on another floor, needing a change from hers. It wasn't long before my mom and I began to job-share my position. I worked three days and she worked three days, which gave us one overlap day that we worked together. I don't know what it was, but the four of us synched perfectly. We all had certain strengths and weaknesses, and Eva was almost supernatural in her ability to delegate accordingly. We all knew I wasn't the one to call when inventory needed to be done—way too overwhelming and understimulating. My brain screeched to a stop just walking into the storage room. If I had to actually count everything in there, it would probably just shrivel up and die. Nor was I the girl to call when copies needed to be made. I never, ever got the staples in the right place. You had to put it in the copier a certain way, but I never thought about it. Even while looking at the stapled copies, I would never think "Hmm….are the staples at the correct angle?" I just couldn't hold that information in my head, for some reason. Eva was only annoyed the first twenty or so times I came back with cockeyed staples. After that, it was so ridiculous that it was kind of funny. I was fortunate that Eva overlooked those things in life that I was less-than-blessed in, and gave me major props for those things I excelled in. I thrived in that environment; I respected her, loved her, and wanted to work hard for her. We liked to say that we played hard and worked harder. We all worked our asses off, but we laughed them off faster! I can't tell you how many times I said something inappropriate in front of the president, causing him to blush, with Eva groaning "Staaaaaacey!" *What?*

Fortunately for me, the president had a great sense of humor, which of course just encouraged me to bring it out. I've always been a bit of a practical joker, and a corporate environment does absolutely nothing to subdue that. I once took his chair out of his office and replaced it with a horrendously straight wooden chair, leaving a note that *my chair was becoming uncomfortable, so I went ahead and switched* with him. I got some good giggles from him on that one, but not all of my shenanigans on our floor were met with applause and appreciation—like the April Fool's Day that I sent Monica, the administrative assistant for the SVP of Legal, an e-mail from "security" stating that they were aware that she had been looking up male child porn on her work computer, or the time Eva told me to add something to my "book," which was meant to keep track of important items related to running the office, and I turned around, flipped her off, and told her to add "this" to her book. I think that may be the only time she actually got mad at me, and even then I was laughing while being reprimanded! I think the worse thing I ever did was to have a security guard in our building (at 2:00 a.m. so they would get out by the deadline the next morning) help me forge the president's signature on a gazillion of his holiday cards after the originals were lost in the mail en route from him to me...though I would call that *innovative* and not mischievous at all!

I made some incredible friends at that job, and there's even a group of us (including my mom, Linda, Eva, Monica, and Mary Ann) that still get together every couple of months or so. Twice a year we're lead by our fearless leader, Marsha from marketing, to a safari ranch owned by her friends. There we unwind from life while we eat, drink, hang out with exotic animals, and get humped by a Labradoodle named Buck until late in the night.

I loved the work and the people, and stayed for three and a half years until Eva decided to retire. I think I was even out the door a couple of weeks before she was, just to make certain that I didn't have to work one day for anyone else. Eva understood me, and that's a rare thing for bosses. I wasn't prepared to go through the whole *caring and feeding of bosses* thing, and with everything happening in my life, I felt like it was a good time to start something new…like manifesting the "download" I had been experiencing for a couple of months. *cue outer space noise*

Chapter 11

I can honestly say I've never met a wall I didn't eventually level, and I'm currently placing dynamite under this bitch, so take cover.

The download was going on the same time I was in the midst of an all-out war raging in my life. Many terrible things happened in a short span of time. In short, Eva was diagnosed with cancer (and, thank God, is now in remission), Willow briefly lost her mind to Multiple Chemical Sensitivity, I killed my cat with a linen spray, and my good buddy McLovin moved away. It was a hard, fast-occurring battle with shit flying everywhere, but my personal growth was also accelerated, which of course I wasn't able to appreciate until it was all said and done. As you can tell, I lived through it, and shit actually washes right out of your hair.

Yoga was my weapon and saved my ass in more ways than one, as it also just happened to get rid of the "underbutt" that had recently shown up below my cheeks. As the proverbial shit was hitting the fan, I was finishing my two-hundred-hour yoga teacher training. When I say *finishing*, I mean everything except for the book report I was supposed to turn in and didn't (it was even completed, but I was so over my head in everything going on, my brain refused to even think about it), and the Ayurvedic cleanse I was supposed to do, which simply didn't happen because Willow had been in the hospital and I didn't have the extra three hundred dollars lying around. Of course, those small discrepancies left me ineligible to become a certified teacher, but I really didn't care. I never went in wanting to teach, I was just desperate to learn. I met my Yogi, Karen, when my mom and I were taking a yoga class at the local recreation center. She was flower-child beautiful and the embodiment of serenity, strength, and grace all at once. Since chaos resided in my brain on a permanent basis, I desperately wanted to visit that place of calm, if only in spurts, and after spending time in her class, I knew yoga was the way to get there. There's a saying, "When the pupil is ready, the teacher will appear," and Karen just so happened to own a yoga teacher training school. She invited me to become her student for a deeply discounted price. I jumped at the chance, warning my mom that I was diving in headfirst, and was prepared to make deep, personal transformations. I think I was actually warning myself. I could feel massive change looming around the corner, but I had no idea of the magnitude and was a fool to think it had to do strictly with intense yoga education. I don't consider it a coincidence that I was finishing my training as I was about to begin battle. Thanks to Karen and yoga, I fought and eventually won the war with that same calm, strength, and grace I never in my life imagined I could carry. I did beat myself up several months afterwards for not turning in my book report and getting that sense of completion, but my mom was there to remind me that everything I needed from yoga I already had in my possession.

You may have noticed that there seem to be a lot of projects I quit right before completion. Let's be honest—a headless man could see that, but I'm not sure what it stems from. Am I afraid of success? Am I afraid of being without a project to stress about? Am I lazy? I'll take the easy way out and say it's probably a combination of all of the above. As my mom likes to tell me, when I don't have stress, I create it. Her theory is that, good or bad, it keeps me stimulated. I tend to agree with her, but for whatever reason that whole completion thing is a killer to mentally push through. A good example is this book you're reading. I've saved writing this entire *work* section for last, because it's the most boring to have to mentally re-live, and I'm having a hell of a time getting through it. I'm miserable. I've been writing these few paragraphs for weeks and it's not like it's extra-good writing because it's taken me so long; it's actually sub-par, and I'm trying to make it decent! It's like a concrete wall that I'm trying to kick down with slippers on. The wall doesn't move, but my feet are no less than mangled! I've literally been banging my head against the wall behind me. I don't know if I'm trying to shake some words loose or knock myself the fuck out of my misery. It's a bitch to go through, but I know the rules by now: keep pushing. Bang my head, pick my nose, throw myself to the floor, whatever I have to do to keep pushing. I know at some point that wall will come down! I can honestly say I've never met a wall I didn't eventually level, and I'm currently placing dynamite under this bitch, so take cover.

The other stuff is for that book I have no intention of writing (I might change my mind when I forget the misery), but I do need to touch on the whole "killing my cat with a linen spray" thing, as it was the most prominent catalyst for the mind-numbing download I was telling you about. For some crazy reason, I was actually making my bed one day, when I decided to get real fancy and spray some of the linen spray I had recently received as a gift. *Pshh. Pshh. Pshh.* Our kitten, Kita, jumped up on the bed not a second later and stood there as the mist fell around him. He gave a few kitty snorts and sneezes before I whooshed him out of the room. Thirty minutes later, Willow and I walked into the kitchen to find him face first on the kitchen floor, with a puddle of saliva around his mouth. I yelled his name and ran over to him, scooping him up in my arms. He was gasping for air for a few seconds, and then it was over. He died in my arms. In retrospect, I'm thankful that I was holding him when he died, instead of him being alone with his little kitty face mashed into the hardwood floor, but at the time I freaked out. Willow was screaming her face off, and I was crying and talking to myself, trying to figure out where to lay his furry body down. My brain was obviously in the *off* position as I walked in circles around the house, pacing for a good five minutes before finally deciding the best idea was surely to lay him on the counter where I prepare my family's food. Thanks for that one, brain!

The vet couldn't tell me what happened unless he did an autopsy, and he couldn't guarantee he would find a cause. It was very expensive and not likely to bring Kita back from the great beyond, which is all I really wanted. I got on the computer and began doing obsessive research to try to figure out how he died. My mind just kept going back to the linen spray. I could not fill my brain with enough information. Everything I read took its place in the holistic view of the picture I was uncovering and absorbing. I learned that essential oils can be extremely toxic to cats, and this particular spray had the essential oils of rosemary and mint (not to be confused with a fragrance— which is just gross chemicals invading your body and tricking your nose into thinking it smells like the name). He was also the runt, just a little thing, so that didn't help his cause. I finally came to the conclusion that as a runt and a cat, his liver was just not able to process and detox those oils, so they basically poisoned him. A spray from a massive bath chain just killed my cat! How many other people are out there spraying this stuff around their animals? In the midst of my frantic research, I couldn't believe the list of items that kept coming up as toxic to animals that I had no idea about! Macadamia nuts? Grapes? Raisins? I'd always considered myself a savvy pet owner. What a joke. I didn't know any of this stuff! At the same time, I was uncovering loads of information about the toxicity of chemicals in pets. My dog Stormi had been suffering from terrible skin allergies for a couple of years, and had been receiving steroid shots accordingly. I was terrified when I read what those steroids were doing to her body, and not only that, they only kept the sores at bay for a month before they reappeared and she would have to get another shot. Clearly we weren't taking care of the source of the problem. In my research, I kept coming across a local holistic vet named Dr. Shawn Messonnier. I decided to take Stormi in to see him about her allergies. He was awesome. He looked at every prescription, every shampoo, everything we had been using, and put them in keep or toss piles. He told us to get her on an all-natural diet (I was such a moron—I thought I was doing well by giving her the most expensive food in the grocery store!), fish oil supplements, an immune support tablet, and voilà, that girl was cleared up in less than two weeks. She has never had allergies or skin problems again. I was stunned, and the ol' brain started kicking into high gear. I thought about how many pets were suffering from miserable allergies and dying early from steroids simply because they weren't on an all-natural food. The humanitarian in me could not bear the thought, and I knew it was time to start sharing the information I was uncovering. *Incoming*! And so started the long and extremely painful download and assimilation. It was months and months of agony as I scribbled on huge notepads, while ideas slammed around in my brain. When I'm in that mode, I feel like I'm not all there. It's like my soul leaves my body to go get some shit done. Running a few errands, maybe faxing something, or warming up coffee…I don't know. I *do* know that things are going on around me in the universe. I can feel it. A fluster and bluster of activity whipping around me like the dirt and dust that surrounds Pigpen. When I had finished downloading, I was so overwhelmed by all of the information I had received, I couldn't even talk about it at all for three months. It was crazy. I felt like I was in *Close Encounters*, sitting at the kitchen table creating sculptures from my mashed potatoes. There were many pieces that made up the concept of the entire idea, but I finally succeeded in putting them all together. At the end of the day, it was an overwhelming picture.

Since my main goal was to share information, I began with a website, paws-forpeace.com, which included a library of articles written by professionals in the field of holistic pet health. It had a database of information that allowed pet owners to look up common pet conditions, and then explained ways to treat those conditions naturally. Dr. Shawn agreed to be my holistic vet advisor and share his volumes of knowledge with my users. When I got that site up, I then created an online directory of vets that was searchable by zip code. Each listing had a logo, information about the vet, a coupon, and a map link to get directions. I called this site pawsforinfo.com. The idea was to charge the vets to be listed in the directory, which would, in turn fund my next project, a nonprofit called Paws for Peace. The nonprofit was designed to supply free holistic health supplies to animal shelters. There are a lot of homeopathic remedies that can be used with shelter animals instead of just shooting them up with chemicals. I was also concerned about the stress the animals were under from living in a shelter environment, and wanted to provide things like flower essences to add to the water bowls for relieving anxiety, and calming CDs to play at night. As I said, these items were to be offered free of charge, on one condition—the shelter had to agree to send a flyer home with every new pet owner directing them to both of the sites. The extra traffic would increase our ability to educate pet owners about holistic pet health, and also create new clients for the vets that agreed to be in our directory, which was ideal, because those vets were the people responsible for funding the aid to the shelters. It was a beautiful, seamless circle, where everyone came out a winner. Though it made sense in the end, those pesky downloads never filter down in any sort of order. Downloads come in the form of little puzzle pieces that I move around and around in my head until I finally start seeing a pattern. Going through a download and then processing it is a bit hardcore, but also a pretty incredible process to watch. I definitely consider it to be one of my superpowers, and something I would never give up just to have a normal brain!

Dave's dad loved the idea and gave us ten thousand dollars to get it started. It was a massive project, and took me months of processing and loads of sketching scribbles, pictures, and ideas in large notebooks. If someone were to look at my notebooks, it would seem like there was something not quite right going on upstairs, but it all made sense to me. When I finally had it all on paper, I moved through each piece of the puzzle, creating as I went. I taught myself html. I taught myself MySQL. I taught myself PHP. You don't know what that stuff is? Well, I didn't either! I was obviously in possession of another person's brain, because I learned, absorbed, and implemented things that people later told me can take years to learn. I did it all in less than six months. The project was enormous, and I could barely get out of my head long enough to communicate with the outside world. I was busy creating the sites, creating the directory, creating the programs, programming, and more programming. Of course, I can't remember any of it now, but at the time, I was Bill Gates, Jr.! Welcome to another of my superpowers: the ability to understand and excel at anything I put my mind to. That is, as long as my mind is interested or motivated. If not...

well, we all know how that turns out. When I finally had all of the Paws for Peace pieces converted from ether to the physical plane, I recruited Dave, Carrie, and McLovin to help me make it a reality. Dave was in charge of the sales of the vet directory, Carrie was in charge of the nonprofit shelter program, McLovin was in charge of steering, and I was the one with the pedal to the metal…the accelerator. Oh yeah, McLovin was also in charge of the brakes, and would use them when I got too far ahead of myself, which in the beginning he did far too often for my taste, but we finally came to a happy medium. Since my tendency was to ignore the brakes completely and his was to ride them like a seventy-eight-year-old grandpa, working together we eventually found the perfect speed.

I thought the creation and implementation of the idea was going to be the most difficult part, but I was wrong. It was the maintenance of all the individual pieces that was the bitch, and was eventually responsible for bringing chunks of the puzzle down in flames. I take full responsibility. I'm a poor delegator and an even worse leader. Because we hadn't yet started making money from this venture, I was embarrassed to ask the crew to do the jobs they signed up for. Nobody knew what they were supposed to be doing, so I tried to do everything, which was impossible, so we kind of spun our wheels, never really taking off in any direction. Dave never got the advertising program off the ground, and neither did the couple of salespeople we hired. There was no way I was getting near anything sales related due to my horrendous social anxiety, and eventually that aspect of the idea was put on the back burner. At the same time, we were coming across issues with shelters, in that they were more in need of basic essentials like food, towels, sheets, and cleaning supplies rather than audio therapy, flower essences, or homeopathic remedies. Without the vet directory sales, we didn't have the funding to buy anything, and though it broke my heart, I had no choice but to put that piece on the back burner as well. I had spread myself too thin and as a result was accomplishing nothing at all. I decided to focus on the original concept and spark, which was to educate pet owners about the benefits of natural health with the Paws for Peace site. No advertisers, no money, no problems. About a thousand monkeys jumped off my back when I came to the conclusion that when I add the idea of generating revenue to something I'm passionate about, it completely takes the fun out of it.

Unfortunately life lessons don't always stick around in my brain, so that whole *no money* thing didn't last long. I had another idea, and this time I recruited my brother to help me. I had a lot of experience bossing him around, so we joined together and started the Boots Loves Biggins line of all-natural shampoos and aromatherapy dog sprays and Peace, Love & Clean, a line of all-natural cleaning supplies, both powered with essential oils. I would do all of the marketing and advertising, and Chris's job was to make the products and recruit and maintain wholesale accounts. I created a shop on Etsy.com, and it did really well. We also acquired some wholesale accounts, and started getting our products in stores. Just as we started to really see some good business, we hit a familiar wall. Chris had to back out of the sales. Unfortunately, he also had a real job, and took a promotion that included inheriting the third shift, meaning when he wasn't working, he was sleeping. That didn't leave a lot of room for selling our stuff, so again, it fell into my lap. I gave it a good run, but with everything else I had going on, and my inability to keep track of and organize anything at all, I was just unable to maintain it by myself, and placed it on the already full back burner. It was incredibly frustrating. I was desperate to be successful at something, and knew it would never happen without a good, old-fashioned, right-hand man—one whose strengths were my weaknesses, and could follow through and take off with my grand ideas. I just want to have the flash of brilliance, get it all going, and then pass it on to someone else to maintain. I want to be involved in only the exciting parts, thank you very much. Not because I'm lazy, but because my strengths happen to lie in those fun parts. If my strengths were in the boring parts, I would do those! It's true! It's not about being where the party is, but rather where I can personally shine, doing exceptional work in whatever project I'm working on. You never see Superman swimming underwater to save the day…that's Aquaman's gig, and not at all a strength of Superman's! You catch my drift; when you're busy saving the world, you stick with what you're good at to get the job done right.

My Brother

Chris, on one of our nature excursions.
He doesn't think he has ADH(D)D, but he's
exactly like me - well, not quite as cool, but
almost. Too bad he's so ugly.

I kept my word, continuing to maintain the Paws for Peace site, and even participated with a booth in some big pet events. As we started nudging into the Smartphone age, I came to the conclusion that I needed to expand from a website to an iPhone app. I already had a Facebook and Twitter presence, so, in my mind, an app was the next logical step. Thanks to another download from beyond, the entire layout and design was already preloaded in my head. I could see every detail, and just needed to extract from my brain to paper, so I created tons of charts documenting what I was seeing in my head. Superpower indeed, but I knew there would still be a couple of hurdles I'd need to kick over to accomplish my newest project. Number one: I would need to sell the idea to Dr. Shawn. You'd think it would be a brainless decision on his part, but he would have to write all of the content, which would take a lot of his time, and he was very busy. Number two: I would need to find a developer that would agree to do it for a percentage of the profits instead of getting paid up front. At the time it was going to cost about thirty-five hundred dollars for the development, and I barely had five hundred dollars in my account. It took me about three different conversations to convince Dr. Shawn that my idea was a good one. By *good* I mean profitable. I had finally secured a developer that had agreed to the terms, and that last tidbit is what finally sold Dr. Shawn on the idea. I had a deal in the making, and I was going forward with him if he agreed, or another vet if he didn't. I really wanted

Dr. Shawn to do it, but I wasn't going to let anything kill my idea. I told you; when *The Force* kicks in, there's absolutely no stopping me, and most times I can't even stop myself.

I knew that in order to be successful, I would need my trusty business sidekick (aka steering and brakes, aka McLovin) along for the ride. Thank God for McLovin. At the time, I had no idea how bumpy and uncomfortable that ride would be. The development process was not a pretty one, and the developers and I rarely saw eye to eye. Legal messes, contracts, missed deadlines, ugly artwork. The list goes on and on, but it finally got so bad that one of the owners eventually refused to speak or work with me any longer. I'll admit, I'm a perfectionist, and won't stand for less. McLovin thought I was being a little too passionate in my e-mails to the developers, so I finally started sending the drafts to him first, so he could edit out the passion that I couldn't filter. It definitely improved my relationship with the developers, but the entire process can be summed up as a nightmare. When the app, *Dr. Shawn's Natural Pet Therapies* was at last published and available on iTunes, we all kind of hugged it out, and it's been fine since.

As you know, after a big project, I tend to go into a funk that can last until I find another adventure to stress about, and after the app, I found myself participating in the most ridiculous adventures by far. For some reason, I came up with the brilliant idea to start poking around in TV and film again. I started auditioning for parts, and for some wacky reason, landed most everything I tried out for. Some of the experiences were really fun, but some were a beating. Did you know there's a whole group of people out there that make a living by being extras? I have no idea why, because being an extra sucks! I once spent twelve hours freezing my ass off in the middle of winter so I could walk back and forth on sidewalks and across streets for the NBC show *Chase*. If the frigid weather didn't suck, the $8.50 an hour pay did, and *everyone* was "writing a screenplay," with an attitude to match! It was incredibly boring, and I finally just got burned out when I kept running into the same self-absorbed people at different gigs. *You're not Kevin Smith, asshole!*

You're an extra, so take it down a notch, m'kay? I actually think the auditions were more exciting than some of the roles, because they were always a little crazy, weird, and stressful. Here's my response to a friend's inquiry about one of the last auditions I went on:

> I had to wear sunglasses while pretending to be blind. I had to walk with a make-believe cane while pretending to be blind. I had to hang my head out of a make-believe car while pretending to be blind. I had to touch the face of a make-believe guy while pretending to be blind. I had to play a real guitar while pretending to be blind. Finally, I had to take off my sunglasses and "appear" blind. I've tried numerous times to look in the mirror and check out the "blind look" that I gave the casting folks, but unfortunately, my version of "appearing" blind involved my eyeballs fixed in the direction of the sky, so I'll never know if I actually looked blind or just really surprised.

I've finally come to the conclusion that what I want to do "when I grow up" will be a constantly evolving idea, and I simply have to evolve with it. That way, when it's all said and done, I will have done everything I've ever wanted to do, instead of wasting time and energy focusing on finding that one elusive thing that will never appear. I'm not just saying that because I've started twenty-seven businesses in my lifetime, either! Yeah…I swear. It's not even an exaggeration. I counted once. Twenty-seven…and that was a couple of years ago, so add five or six on to that number! Obviously, most of them failed due to my loss of interest or inability to do the grunt work, but Dave told me the other day how much he respects my ability to constantly put myself in the face of failure and then gracefully fail. I think it's because I just don't consider failure as failure…it's more of a lesson, and there's nothing I love more than learning, so I can't imagine any other way to spend my time. One of these days I'll find that right-hand man I was talking about, and become a mini-mogul…free to save the entire world with the money I'm determined to make, yet find so offensive.

Section Four:
Relating to Humans

"I love you, and because I love you, I would sooner have you hate me for telling you the truth than adore me for telling you lies."

—Pietro Aretino

Chapter 12

I'd be like a ninja, in then out, claiming diet and exercise as the reason for my newly svelte shape!

I've dreaded this moment, writing about relationships. I'm just not sure where to start. I'd like nothing more than to sit here and give you little glorious bits of humorous wisdom on how to make the relationships in your life work…I really would. I just can't, though, because I don't know how. I don't know anything about holding on to and nurturing relationships. It's pretty bad, and I'm ashamed. I actually beat myself up about it a lot, which changes nothing. I still don't have what it takes. It reminds me of when Jennifer Aniston said that Brad Pitt was "missing a sensitivity chip." I totally get that, and I think I may even be missing the same chip!

I've left a path a mile wide of people I've hurt by my seemingly insensitive actions. I forget birthdays. I detest talking on the phone. I'm not affectionate…blah, blah, blah. I didn't go visit a friend in the hospital after her gastric bypass surgery and hurt her feelings so badly she got onto me. Honestly, it never even crossed my mind…just like most things. It isn't that I am deliberately being insensitive; it's just that sometimes things don't occur to me. It's not like there was an action that I just chose *not* to take, it just never even entered my freaking brain! What am I supposed to do with that? Besides, it's not like she was in an accident, or had emergency surgery or a baby—she chose the surgery and chose to be there! I guess in my cluttered brain that didn't warrant a visit, and besides that, if the situation were switched, I wouldn't want anyone visiting me! I'd be like a ninja—in then out—claiming diet and exercise as the reason for my newly svelte shape!

I always find myself in those debacles. The absolute worst happened not too long ago. Our good friends invited Dave and me to a birthday celebration in my girlfriend's honor. Her husband had gotten a suite at a fancy hotel and made elaborate plans for the night. Long story short, the evening didn't turn out as planned. They ended up getting in a huge fight at the restaurant, and it only escalated when we got back to the suite, so he finally just left the hotel in a huff, acquiring a broken hand on the way out from punching the wall during his dramatic exit. She was left, stunned and alone, sitting on the couch bawling her eyes out. It was awful, and I sat next to her trying to give her some kind of comfort. Dave and I spent the night with her in the suite so she wouldn't have to be alone in her fancy hotel on her birthday. At the time, it never occurred to me that I may have been falling short on the friend duties that night. I had never heard of the *hug* rule.

Later that month, I was visiting my friends in Wichita. The app had come out, and I was in that post-project funk that I can't stand. It makes me crazy that I do that, but I think I just put so much energy and hyper-focus into my projects that by the time they end, I'm depleted of most of my life force. I have to withdraw from the world to gain some of my energy back. That's also the reason I can't take on long-term projects. I am physically unable to put forth a massive amount of energy for an extended amount of time. I would say that a month is the longest I can go on a project and still stay healthy. After that the project becomes a monster, and I go to battle every day, using up energy I don't have, to fight completing it. As it was, it had been a three-month-long project, and I was in the usual dead place with my hands covering my head trying to protect my vulnerable self that barely held a flicker of life.

Even on my best day, I'm introverted and suffer from social anxiety. Sitting at Carrie's that night, you can imagine my despair when she announced that her neighbors were going to come over to drink some beer. When you're hanging out in the dead place, the last thing you want to do is meet new people and try to be bubbly. It's impossible. I didn't have enough in me to pull it off. As soon as the words left her lips, I felt the tears start burning my eyes. It was so irrational, but such a punch in the gut, I couldn't help it. Carrie was mortified. She hadn't in ten years of knowing me ever seen me cry (she said she may have heard me cry on the phone once regarding a pumpkin-carving contest we were going to have that she tried to reschedule). I was equally mortified, saying, "I don't know why I'm crying".

She looked at me, looked down, looked back at me, and said, "Am I supposed to hug you?" Awkward silence.

"No!" I whispered emphatically. She wiggled in her seat.

"Well, I didn't think so, but I thought I should ask since you're always supposed to hug someone if they're crying." I immediately stopped sniffling as I had an instant flashback of my friend sitting on the couch, in her fancy birthday suite, crying. Sure, I tried to comfort her, but I never hugged her! I was supposed to hug her? I didn't know there was a rule that you were always supposed to hug someone if they're crying!

I looked at Carrie, panicking. "Always?" I yelled. "You're *always* supposed to hug someone if they're crying? I didn't know that rule!" She was looking at me with her mouth open.

"How do you not know that rule?"

"Nobody told me!" I could tell she thought I was finally losing it, so I hurriedly gave her the short version of the story and, to my utter dismay, she agreed that I had totally fucked up by not hugging my poor friend. I was completely mortified by my inaction. Those are the kind of times when I wish I was more normal and that basic social cues, like hugging a friend when they're crying, came more naturally to me. It all goes back to "it never occurred to me." Would I want someone to hug me if I were crying? Not at all. Which is why, I assume, it never crossed my mind that someone *would* want to be hugged.

Suddenly withdrawing or moving on without notice or explanation is my MO in a relationship. To be fair, in my mind, the notice has already been given. Just so you know, when I say *relationship*, I mean relating to other people, no matter who it is. Friend, lover, spouse, co-worker, whatever. For me there's no difference. The only thing I go by is if there's a connection and if it works or doesn't. I don't want it to sound like I'm mean or nasty. I'm a really nice person, and I can have superficial relationships with most anyone, but there are very few people that know me on a deeper level, and I guard that space with my life. Few individuals have the backstage pass to Stacey (that doesn't sound right). It takes years to get there, and most don't last longer than six months trying. I have always tried to analyze why I can't seem to foster lasting relationships, and sometimes wonder if I'm not just lazy! I just don't want to have to take the time to explain myself and my kooky ways. *Sure we can be friends, but here is a long disclaimer to read and sign before you decide to embark on this adventure. To sum it up, it states that there's a 99 percent chance that you'll be hurt in this relationship, as I will most likely disappoint you first and then hit the road, leaving you confused, hurt, and bitter. Your bitterness will actually begin before I leave, but after you realize that I am not the bright, shiny star you knew for the first three months...that "supernova," as my friend, Mary Ann, calls it. Thanks to my radar, I'll eventually start to feel that bitterness and disappointment in me seeping from your pores when I talk to you or see you, and that's when I'll start packing my bags. Shortly thereafter, I'll be gone.* That's not exactly a welcome wagon to friendship. You can see why it's easier for me to stay distant. Nobody gets hurt, and I don't have to feel the shame. That's what you call a win-win in my book! Just the other day, after a horrific bout with the dead place, and repercussions from friends and family that come from going there, Mary Ann sent me an e-mail that read, "Well, I'm climbing out of this place (again) and I'm sure it won't be the last time. I'm so grateful for your words. Members of my own family have said I'm a 'horrible person,' because I 'shut them out.' Some friends, the ones who say things like, 'Life is too short, get over it' and 'Take your meds' and claim I'm seeking attention with my pathetic loser ways…they are not really on my radar, but their words stick with me. Funny. So I seek new people who I haven't alienated and who think my bubbly bursts of energy and fearlessness are charming. Those who I haven't let down yet. Those who haven't seen me as dark matter but only supernova. Ha ha. suckers." I couldn't have said it better myself.

Fortunately, the universe is usually on my side, and the truly special relation-ships I do manage to maintain all seem to have fallen out of the sky and right into my lap. The best part is the tag attached that says "maintenance free." In smaller letters it states, "This individual will not only *accept* you, but abso-lutely *adore* you for who you are." Hot dog! I'll take a dozen of those!

On the outside, I'm a pretty bubbly person and growing up I never had a hard time making friends. I can remember the names of all of my best friends in each state I lived in, and am now in touch with most of them again, thanks to Facebook. Moving to Kansas (and actually staying for a while) forced me to learn how to not only develop those friendships, but maintain them. I must have done something right (actually, I have to give credit to my friends, as they are my anchors) because two of my best friends now are the same I had in fifth grade. Though over the years, I sometimes paddle out to meet new people and experience new things, when it inevitably sinks, I am always able to paddle back to Christa and Donya. They have never pulled that anchor up and left me. That feeling of security is precious, and I'm pretty sure I don't show them or tell them enough how much it continues to mean to me over the years.

As I mentioned, I met Carrie when I was working at the market research firm. She was taking Bob's class, and was hired as a caller in our call center, quickly moving up to the manager position. She was usually coming as I was going, so we never really spoke. A few months after she started, I was work-ing on a huge project, where I needed to mystery shop a local bank and all of its branches. Unfortunately, I needed a person to go with me, so we could do both drive-through and in-store transactions. Fortunately, my bosses asked Carrie. After driving around for hours together in the car, we bonded over our mutual love of marijuana…and the rest, as they say, is history. Carrie is the bubble in my champagne of life. As luck would have it, Christa and Donya, champagne lovers they are, were able to see what I saw and welcomed Carrie into our little friendship circle. I remember getting in the moving truck, and waving good-bye to the three of them as I headed west to San Diego, feeling so happy they all had each other. Ten years later they all live in Wichita, and along with Christa's younger sister, Mandy, remain the best of friends and get together quite often. I love going to visit those girls. They are so incredibly supportive, and have a knack for making me feel good when I want to feel bad about myself. We pick up where we left off every time. Dave calls them the *Real Housewives of Wichita*.

I once went to a psychic/medium gallery, where a bunch of people sit in a room and the medium randomly connects with the energy of the audience member he or she is reading. To my elation, I was chosen to be read, and after looking at me for a bit in silence, the psychic told me he felt confusion, and as if he was looking at two different people. Great…a bipolar diagnosis from a psychic. Unfortunately, I completely knew what he was talking about because I truly feel that way sometimes. Not that I'm bipolar, but that I'm two people, and not just two people, but two people at odds with each other. The mom and the kid, the homebody and the explorer, the strong and the weak, the logical and the emotional, the funny and the sad, the angry and the calm, the open and the closed, the loved and the hated, the hot and the cold, the alive and the dead, the beautiful and the ugly. It's exhausting. I. Am. Exhausting.

As I said before, my brain is like the accelerator on a car—a car without brakes or a steering wheel. Kind of like Fred Flintstone, but worse…I think he has a cement steering wheel if I'm not mistaken. I have no steering wheel, and would welcome even one made of cement. My husband is so insanely supportive, he doesn't dare try to steer me. When I crash, which I inevitably do, he just picks me up, dusts me off, and sends me on my way. That's why he's my husband. No shame, no judgment. That's how we roll, which is incredibly necessary when we're talking about my personal life…it works. We would be miserable otherwise. But when it comes to business, the out-of-control car is just not able to maintain a consistent steady speed, or even stay on the damn road, which makes it pretty much impossible to reach the desired destination. That, and I always wait until the gas light comes on to fill up the tank.

As I was saying, my most important relationships fall from the sky like a cosmic gift. I was working for Eva when I met my brain wrangler (not to be confused with the Hamburglar) You know him as McLovin.

McLovin and I worked on different floors. Whenever he had a reason to come up, he would pop by my cube. He would actually pop by every cube on the floor, as he couldn't pass through without being called over by most everyone. I called him "The Mayor." Everyone loved him. The guys liked him because he was smart, sarcastic, and clever. The girls liked him because he was charming, good looking, and English…at least, on the outside. On the inside, well, he's actually still English, but he's also fighting his own dual-persona battle. Bless his heart, *his* internal battles are pretty violent and never without mental blood, guts, gore, and casualties. Take right now, for instance. We usually speak on the phone a couple of times a week. We haven't spoken in three months. He won't return my calls or e-mail. It sucks, but I'm not offended, because I know that he's in the dead place, trying to claw his way out. He goes there, too. That's why we understand each other.

I didn't really get to know McLovin as a person, and not just The Mayor, until we made a bet against each other one day. I don't remember what the actual bet was. All I know is that he lost and the result was he had to call me "Queen" for a week. I think he called me Queen for two days, and then we both forgot, but the friendship remained. After that, we would go get coffee every now and then. I loved picking his brain. We talked about everything from fate and destiny to quantum mechanics. I really looked forward to our conversations because I always felt smarter after talking to him. Not because of his accent, though I do like to tell him he only sounds smart because of it, but because he has a way of explaining things to me in that nonlinear way that my brain can actually understand…and…OK…I'll admit, accent or not, he's a pretty smart dude.

As the stupid saying goes, all good things must come to an end, and later that year McLovin told me he was packing up his wife and three kids for a move to Florida and a new position within the company. I was pretty bummed out. I was going to miss feeling smart. With promises to keep in touch, he left in January. A few months later, I ended up leaving the company with Eva's retirement. Since relationships normally float in and out of my life like ghost ships, it never occurred to me that McLovin and I would actually stay in touch, but somehow we did, phone phobia and all.

When I was finally able to process my Paws for Peace idea, I knew without a doubt that I needed to recruit McLovin to help me guide the U.S.S. Crazy. I was afraid to ask him, as he was traveling to a different country every week, and I knew he was overwhelmed and busy with work and his family. He was also a really nice guy who wouldn't want to hurt anyone's feelings, and I didn't want a "pity" yes, but I knew in my gut that we were supposed to be in business together. I knew we were a match made in successful-business heaven. Where I'm hurried, he's paced; where I'm frantic, he's calm; and where I'm negligent, he's cautious. We have as many similarities as we do differences, but he brings me into balance, and I'd like to think I do the same for him—after all, who wants to only be paced, calm, and cautious all the time? Boring!

One day when he called to check in, I bravely gathered my guts from the floor where they lay and pooped (a typo, and it stays) the silly question to him. "Will you be the COO [we only held titles for one day, as it was so stupid and embarrassing] to Paws for Peace?" He laughed really hard and then agreed. Since then, he has spent the last five years of his life keeping me from crashing (for the most part) with a quirky smile on his face, and not a dime to show for it. Actually, that's not true. We did make some money from the app he helped me develop, but it's still sitting in the bank account, untouched, because he's currently residing in the dead place, and sorry partner…money just ain't no good in the dead place.

McLovin

The elusive Murk, aka McLovin. This is the only known photo of the two of us together. Fun fact: he wasn't wearing that hat in the photo. I added it for the book because I think I'm funny as hell.

You might be wondering what my husband thinks of this Yin Yang relationship with this other man. Does he get angry? Jealous? Possessive? Nope. My husband adores McLovin as much as I do, and is eternally grateful to him for his ability to keep me focused, feeling understood, and out of his hair. When we all get together, they give me shit all the way to Friday. It warms my heart seeing them laughing as they make fun of me for something. We owe McLovin big time, and one of these days, one of my kooky ideas is going to make those two boys a shit-ton of money, and then they can laugh at me all the way to the bank. That will be my pleasure.

Who is this seemingly perfect husband I keep referring to? Is he really perfect? Actually, no, not at all. As a matter of fact, a couple of weeks ago, he and I came to the conclusion that he has "no common sense." That's not a judgment, my friend…simply an observation. And not just my observation—his, too! Funny how that never crossed our minds when he accidentally packed the cat in a box and stored her in the garage (she lived to meow about it). I have many examples of the same kind of stupid. I'm not sure what the catalyst was, but once we finally figured out that he was simply lacking common sense, and not just plain dumb, I had to cut him some slack. I needed to be as accepting of his brain as he was of mine. I still try to keep that in mind when he does something completely idiotic, and thankfully he returns the favor three-fold.

Ours wasn't your typical boy-meets-girl love story. It was more of a "boy lies to girl"…at least the kind of lies you would tell a chick that you meet in a club in Vegas and expect to never talk to again. He had no idea he was talking to his future wife when he told me that he was a twenty-five-year-old (twenty-two-year-old) kindergarten teacher (student teacher in college) living on a San Diego beach (in the hills) with his friends (parents), and millions of dollars in inheritance (ten thousand dollars) coming to him. Oh yeah, and his best friend, Brent, sitting next to him, was a race-car driver (amateur beach Wiffle ball player).

I was living in Wichita, and at the tail-end of a three-year relationship. I had already moved out of the house we had purchased together just six weeks prior to me leaving. Though living separately, we were still "together," as we half-expected to work things out and then I would give up my temporary residence and move back in. As you know, things change and things don't change. It was the end of 1999, and I was hell-bent on starting 2000 off with a clean slate. I was invited to Donya's wedding, which was taking place in January in Vegas, and I wanted to go as a person that was either single or taken. I would be OK with either; I just needed to be one or the other (all or nothing). It wasn't a popular conversation topic, and things weren't improving, so I finally came to the conclusion and patiently explained to my soon-to-be ex that I would be going to Vegas as a single lady (holla!). How'd he take it? Let's put it this way…he didn't shed any tears.

It's amazing to me how the universe responds when you get rid of things that aren't working in your life. You make room for things that do work, and then they come. It's like magic!

Chapter 13

I'm sure I lost some of my "cool" points when I started spitting neon green saliva on the dance floor after biting through my faux-rave glow stick.

There was a big group of us in Las Vegas for the wedding. It was the night before the ceremony, and we were planning on going out for the bachelorette party. We were trying to decide where to go, and I was uncharacteristically adamant about going to Studio 54. Normally, I'm more of a go-with-the-flow girl. Not that night. I was hell-bent on going to Studio 54. I didn't know crap about Studio 54. Why did I care? My guess is it's because I was a mere two hours away from meeting my future husband at the very same place. As you know, for the most part, I have a really good relationship with my intuition, and when it says to jump, I tend to take a flying leap!

Studio 54 was everything I imagined. There was a line four thousand miles long just to get into the place. I don't know if it's because we were obnoxious or cute, but we were ushered in ahead of the line, which is probably a good thing, because me trying to stand in a line is about as ugly as it gets. From behind me, it would probably appear that I suffer from a seizure disorder. Limbs jutting out in all directions, walking in place, bending over to stretch…ohhhh, it's very hard for me to stand in a line. As we passed through the doorway, we stepped into a dark cavern. It was clammy and neon-cheesy with that horrible club music playing in the background: (cue music) Untz. Untz. Untz. Untz. Untz. "Kill me now. This place sucks. My brain is about to explode from this music! Oh, God! Sensory overload! Help! Oh wait…is that a tray of shots? Let's paaaaarty!" Untz. Untz. Untz. Untz. Untz.

Thank goodness we were all looking relatively attractive that night, because I'm sure I lost some of my "cool" points when I started spitting neon green saliva on the dance floor after biting through my faux-rave glow stick. I was determined to get every ounce of that glow-in-the-dark cocktail out of my mouth right there where I was standing. Not because it was most likely filled with swamp-gas-like chemicals, but simply because I didn't want to scare the piss out of every guy in the joint when I flashed a smile filled with Toxic Avenger teeth (Dave ended up being a witness to that unfortunate incident… and he still married me. What a champ!).

That whole cluster must have been going on the same time the "cage people" were lowered from the ceiling while gyrating above us. I only assume this because my face was toward the floor for a while, spitting. Even with the unfortunate spitting ordeal over with, I still never noticed the cage people above me or the half-naked people being lowered by chains next to them. The only reason I ever found out they existed was because I saw them in the party pictures much later, after returning home. I remember flipping through Donya's photos, completely confused by their looming presence above me, as I'm pictured posing next to Dave, with glow-in-the-dark, neon-green saliva strings hanging from my mouth.

You know what? I'm getting ahead of myself. I need to start from the beginning, or I'll get completely confused. It happens a lot. Sometimes, if I go into a store, I have to start on one side and work my way to the other. I prefer stores with actual rows, as it helps me establish my pattern. That gives this funky brain of mine some room to actually look at items in a store. It doesn't have to stress about where to walk next, so I can use that brainpower to, *ta-da!*, F-O-C-U-S. At least, that's what it feels like to me. That's a long-winded way of saying I don't have to work to create a logical beginning to a logical end, so I can just enjoy the ride. Bueller? OK, at this point, I've probably lost you, so let me just take you back to earlier that night...

I had just started doing shots to try to drown the sensory overload I was going through. If I didn't relax soon, a facial tic was sure to join the party. To top it off, I had been really having problems with Irritable Bowel Syndrome (IBS), and I never knew when I would have to rush to the bathroom, silently cursing the greasy cheese pizza I had eaten earlier that day at New York! New York! Of course, if there's anything worse than grease for IBS, it's alcohol. I was maxing out on both, so I was like a loaded weapon just waiting to unleash my fury in the nearest casino bathroom stall.

Let me pause for a second to tell you that I once ripped a fabric belt right off my waist in a desperate and unsuccessful attempt to untie it before I nearly pooped right there on an elevator floor in front of Carrie and the guy trying to get off on the fourth floor. I was ready to have my pants down to my knees before I ever got out of the elevator just to save that precious time...mere milliseconds between me making it and losing every cool point I have ever acquired by crapping right there in the hallway (actually Carrie would give me more points for crapping in the hall, now that I think about it). Needless to say, thanks to my superhuman about-to-shit-my-pants strength, I was able to rip the belt completely in half when I figured out the knot was slowing me down. It was a pretty sweet thing to witness, and the reason I made it on the pot in the nick of time! After I sat down, we couldn't even breathe from laughing so hard. I was just thankful I was sitting on a toilet to avoid the poop equivalent of a murder scene in the front room.

If all of the above doesn't give you a pretty good idea of where my brain was, I don't know what will. I'm not sure what I was looking for at Studio 54 that night, but I'll tell you what I wasn't looking for...love, marriage, or babies in a baby carriage. I just wanted to be single for once. My dating style was to find a guy, try to save him, not feel appreciated, give warning, release any guilt, and finally hit the road. That usually took a couple of years—minimum six months. I was over taking care of other people. I just wanted to take care of myself. "All the Single Ladies!"…ha! That's what I thought! Now I think to myself, "Geez, where'd I get my intuition that night? A nickel and dime store?" I honestly thought I was going to hit a jackpot, not score a husband (does everyone feel like they're going to hit a jackpot when they go to Vegas, or is it just me? I mean, it's never happened, but I'm always convinced it will!)

Back at Studio 54, and with a few drinks under our belts, Christa and I slinked our way across the club to go get a drink or go to the bathroom…I don't really remember where we were headed, and when I say "slink," I mean, as well as a girl with a sensory disorder trying to function in a crazy-loud club with colored lights slamming against her eyeballs (me) and a new mom whose breasts had absolutely no idea she was trying to kick back a little bit in Vegas, and forced her to pump them in random casino bathrooms every two hours (Christa) can slink.

A waitress stopped us as we were making our way to wherever we were going—probably to pump, now that I think about it! I was her pumping companion so she wouldn't have to hang out in strange bathrooms by herself. I did learn a lot about breast pumps. Weird contraptions, those breast pumps. The waitress explained that a table of men bought us drinks, and then motioned behind her. Aww, man! If we take the drinks (as if anything else would have been considered), we would have to go thank them…yuck. Small talk. Hate it. Phooey! I looked past the waitress to see what they looked like. What? I wasn't being shallow! I wanted to make sure they didn't look like serial killers! To my confusion/astonishment/wonder/embarrassment, I thought I was looking at a scene from the movie, *Swingers*. Oh my. The large collared shirts and "money" suits from Men's Wearhouse (discounted even more than normal, as one of the guys worked there), the newly shined shoes, the gelled hair. They were a piece of work. I was disturbed yet curious, and didn't want to seem ungrateful for the drink, so Christa and I nodded to each other and headed over to their table.

There was a gaggle of guys with big collars to greet us as we walked up. They were cute in a trying-too-hard way. I mean, seriously, there is just no acceptable substitute for Vince Vaughn and Jon Favreau, so it almost made me annoyed. We smiled and thanked them for the drinks. After a bit of small talk (despise it), we were turning away to resume our original mission, when one of the guys yelled out, "Where are you from?" Oh man…that question is such a beating if you're from Kansas, because after you reply, you inevitably get the "Where's Toto?" or "We're not in Kansas anymore!" and you can genuinely tell that they think they are the first person to have ever come up with the clever *Wizard of Oz* reference! That just adds another level of annoyance for me.

I looked at the guy, rolled my eyes, and said, "Try to guess."

His response? "Wichita, Kansas!" Did he just say…? My eyes narrowed as I stared at him.

"Do I know you?"

He looked at me bewildered, "No, why?"

"Because I *am* from Wichita, Kansas!" This time his eyes narrowed. I could tell he didn't believe me. And I knew for a fact that none of our group had moseyed this way before us.

He shook his head. "No way. Show me your ID; I don't believe you." As I was getting my ID out, I asked him why he said Wichita, and he said he was just being a smart-ass, because in his kindergarten class that he (student) taught, that week during a geography lesson they had talked about Wichita, Kansas, as the "Air Capital of the World." It was on his mind and random, so he said it. I have a pretty good BS meter, and he seemed to be sincere. After I showed him my license, he couldn't believe it. That must have been a good icebreaker, because Christa and I ended up sitting down and doing shots with them.

That's when my future husband weaved his web of lies for me. Don't get me wrong; I totally get it. You're talking to a girl in Vegas…you want to impress her. It's not like you'll ever see her again, right? Needless to say, it was a pretty interesting next six months watching each white lie unravel as I got to know him better over the phone. As I said, I saw his side, so I didn't care that he had fibbed. It was just fun watching him squirm as he tried to worm his way out.

As you already know, it's kind of a blur after that. I know that I was with this guy "Dave" for the rest of the night. Later, I had to rely on him for details to fill in the blanks. I also knew we had spent a lot of time on the dance floor, and at a table every now and then, taking a break and drinking more (IBS be damned!) before heading back for a dance-off. He tells me that we made out on the dance floor, but to this day, I don't believe him. Number one: I would never make out with somebody that I had just met. If I'm kissing you, it's because I know you enough to like you *and* your germs. Number two: I would never, ever make out in public. I'm a prude and private. Number three may not be as convincing, but I'll give it a shot: I don't remember any such thing. I know, I know. There are quite a few things that I can't recall from that night, but I'm telling you, if I made out with a strange guy in public, I would remember. Hammered or not! Dave says otherwise. I say, where's the proof? Sure, he may have a picture of me dancing with my shirt half up and a dollar bill in my mouth, but that's a different story, which I unfortunately do remember. I think it was close to 2:30 a.m. when our group decided to call it a night. I told Dave good-bye and that I would see him around. We had another two days there, and I was pretty confident I would run into him again before I left.

The next day was the wedding, so we were pretty busy with the final details. I didn't give a lot of thought to Dave, and for the life of me could not remember what he looked like until Christa and I decided to do some sightseeing that afternoon. We actually did end up seeing him, but we were walking down the strip, and Dave and his buddies were all piled in a cab yelling at us as they drove by in the opposite direction. His face was still a mystery.

The ceremony was sweet, and very "Donya." The reception was held in her suite. After photos, cake, and toasting, we moved it to a club somewhere. It was there that the girls informed me that the night before, they had invited Dave and his friends to the club reception. They said he acted like he wanted to check it out. Hmm. I had mixed emotions. I did like him, and I thought it would be fun to hang out, but I also wanted to do my own thing. I wasn't sure I wanted to waste my two nights in Vegas on the same company. I like to mix it up.

There was a group of us on the dance floor when I heard a ruckus from the direction of our big table. I looked over and saw that Dave and his entourage had arrived, so my friends were in a tizzy for me. They pointed him in my direction. *Wow. I forgot he was so tall. Dang. He's pretty cute.* He had a huge smile on his face as he walked over to me on the dance floor. *Butterflies.* When he reached me, he scooped me up in a big hug. OK. Sure. Why not? I'll hang out with him. I can always lose him if I want to.

At some point, later that night, Christa (I love her to this day for being such a good sport and going with me, even with a looming 6 a.m. flight), Dave, his friend, Collin, and I made it out of the club, and headed to the Stratosphere to brave the roller coaster and other rides perched precariously on top of the sky-high tower. Christa and I had been going to amusement parks, fairs, and carnivals together since we were kids, and we were eager to scare the crap out of ourselves (quite possibly literally, in my case). Thankfully, we lived through the rides, and I didn't even poop my pants in front of the guy I was beginning to like. I wasn't sure how much of my bodily fluids he could handle in two days, and I wouldn't have been surprised if a little of the glow-in-the dark fluid had found its way through my system!

After the rides, we sat in a bar talking. Christa hung out for about an hour before she told us she needed to head back to the room, as she had an early flight and needed to pump before bed. I walked her to the room, and then headed back downstairs to hang out with the guys a bit longer.

I found them back in the bar, and asked them if they fancied playing some slots. They informed me they were more "blackjack" kind of guys. I couldn't imagine anyone not loving a nickel slot machine, so I dragged them over and gave them the cup of nickels I had acquired during the past two days. We must have played those slots for two hours. Collin just kept on winning, and I'm proud to say at the end of the night, he announced that he loved nickel slots, and Dave announced *his* love for *me*. After I watched the guys attack a 3 a.m. breakfast of chicken fried steak the size of my head, Collin decided to call it a night. Dave and I went back to the empty bar and continued to get to know each other. I just kept thinking there was something about this guy. I couldn't put my finger on it, but I could definitely tell that something was going on in the universe. At 5 a.m., we headed up to my room to see Christa off to the airport. When we got there, she was, of course, pumping. We stayed in the hallway until she was finished. At this point we had irrational giggling going on due to lack of sleep. Christa finished up and let us in. She was all packed and out the door less than five minutes later. That meant it was only the two of us. Alone. In a hotel room. Thankfully my husband is wired exactly like me, and there was only one thing on both of our minds. Sleep. I'm still not sure everyone believes that nothing happened that night. I remember being quite shocked the next day, when Donya asked me if we had sex. "Of course not! Geesh!" In her defense, she merely said out loud what everyone else was thinking. My mom even asked me eight years later if I had slept with him that night—my own mom! The thing is, if I can't even *kiss* a strange man, do you really think I'm going to get naked with one and let him put *his* body parts in *my* body parts? Absolutely not. It's not even a morals and values thing…it's a germ thing!

We decided to lie on the bed and set the alarm for 7 a.m. Since he was in a suit, I let him borrow a pair of my sweats to lie down in. I had my hands over my eyes as he was changing, but I managed to sneak a peek at his underwear through the space between my fingers. "Oh No! Not tighty-whities!" I'm definitely a "boxer" girl, and since I have no filter, as it ran through my head, it ran out of my mouth. After scolding me for peeking, Dave explained to me that when you're wearing slacks, you need to wear the briefs to keep everything smooth and compact, and assured me that on a day-to-day basis, boxers were the soup du jour. Tragedy diverted! I could now close my eyes and peacefully go to sleep lying next to this strange man who was wearing my pants (on top of the covers, of course).

The alarm went off five minutes later. OK, maybe not five minutes, but it sure felt like it. My eyes felt like an alien probe had removed all of the moisture while I slept. Dave looked like he had eaten a chicken fried steak the size of my head just hours before. We both felt a little shy as we smiled at each other and said Good Morning, trying not to intoxicate each other with our liquor-filled breath. I wanted to sleep for another ten hours, but I had a flight later that day, and I needed to move all of my stuff to Donya's suite and check out of the current room. Dave and his friends were meeting for breakfast forty-five minutes later, and he still had to get to his hotel, which was downtown, to shower and change. We promised to meet up later that morning. My phone wasn't getting good service, so he left me his number, with instructions to call him at 10 a.m. He gave me a peck on the mouth and then walked to the door, not even trying to hide his smile. Again: butterflies. I sat on the bed, slightly dizzy, as the door closed behind him.

With my wits about me once again, I moved my belongings and checked out of the room. By then, it was almost time for me to call Dave, and I needed to find a spot with good reception. I opened my purse to find his number. After searching carelessly for a minute, I decided I needed to focus and take everything out of my purse one by one. I was looking at an empty purse, with the contents scattered around me and no phone number. I checked my pockets, my purse, my pockets, my purse. I thought for sure it would appear if I just kept checking those same spots. I was trying to visualize what the note looked like. He had written it on "Stratosphere" paper, with the "Stratosphere" pen (that I still have). I remembered seeing the number laying on the table, and then nothing of it after that. "Shit. I bet I threw it away." I always clean up my hotel room before I leave (because I care about what the housekeepers think of me, even if I never see their faces), and I remembered throwing a bunch of papers away. Yep…that's where it is, alright. I made a feeble attempt to rescue the number by checking with the front desk to see if my room had been cleaned since I left. As luck can sometimes go, it had been cleaned, and I was screwed.

I did some last-minute shopping as I waited to meet the airport shuttle. I felt bad about the whole phone number thing. For a couple of reasons, but mostly because I didn't want Dave to think that I had stood him up. That idea really bothered me, and I wasn't sure how to remedy that. My only consolation was that I, without a doubt, knew that I would be speaking to him soon, and I'd be able to tell him the story myself. I'm not sure why I was so confident. I didn't have his number, and he didn't have mine, but getting on that airport shuttle, when the driver asked me if I had a good time in Vegas, I replied that indeed I had, smiling widely, knowing full-well that my life was about to change, and it had something to do with Dave, the twenty-five-year-old teacher that lived on the beach with his friends, awaiting his million dollar inheritance (which I didn't care about…what were the odds I would marry this guy, anyway?).

Love "Las Vegas" Style
I had no idea this
man would turn up
as my husband one day.

Chapter 14

I thought for sure it was going to have to do with my excessive drinking or marijuana smoking, as those are the only things he really nagged me about… and occasionally my language, if I was on a roll.

I landed in Wichita later that night. My newly ex'd boyfriend, Brent, picked me up in my car, with our big, yellow Lab, Sibley. When I looked at him and asked where *his* car was, you can imagine how annoyed I was when he told me that we had to stop at a bar downtown and pick it up, as he'd been too drunk to drive it home the previous night. See what I mean? Same shit, different day. If that wasn't enough, we had to get the jumper cables out to get it started when we finally made it to where it was parked. My annoyance turned to full-blown irateness when, in the midst of the chaos trying to get his Jeep started, we locked my keys in my running car with the heater on full-blast, and the dog waiting patiently inside. We called a locksmith. They were out twenty minutes later, but left twenty minutes after that, unsuccessful. I was in a panic, worried that Sibley was going to overheat. I did what any mama would do. I grabbed the tire wrench from the back of the jeep, and began smashing it against the window, as my ex was yelling at me to stop. *Must. Save. My. Baby.*

I was swinging that wrench as hard as I could, and my arm became numb from the reverberation. I had only managed to scratch the tint on the window—a tiny scratch that you would have to look hard for if you wanted to see it.

I handed the wrench to my ex. He took one look at the crazy written all over my face, and started hitting the window as hard as he could. Ten times. Twenty times. Nothing. It wouldn't break. I looked over at him with the wrench in his hand, sweating out last night's liquor, and I knew. It was over. We were over. For good. Even though the fire department had to rescue Sibley (they were able to unlock the door), I was thankful for that chaotic event. The anger was a gift that gave me the strength it took to finally emotionally walk away from a relationship that was no longer working for either one of us.

Three or four days later, I was thinking about Dave, feeling immensely guilty. I'm always worried about a person's feelings, and it made me sick to my stomach to imagine him thinking I stood him up in Las Vegas. I liked Dave. He was good-looking, funny, sweet, and he had manners. How could you stand up a guy like that? Keep that in mind when I tell you what I did next, because otherwise I could sound like a crazy stalker person. I remembered him telling me that his mom worked at UCSD and that her name was Judi. I knew his last name. Would I dare look her up? And, if I did find her, what the hell was I going to say? "Hello Mrs. Turis, you don't know me, but my name is Stacey, and I met your son in Vegas….Can you give me his number?" In a normal situation, I would never put myself through something embarrassing like that, but my guilt was calling the shots, so that's exactly what I did, and that's exactly what I said when she answered the phone.

Her response was immediate. "Are you pregnant?" I could hear the sarcasm in her voice and replied, "No ma'am, we didn't have sex; and even if we did, it would be too soon to tell if I was pregnant, since it was only last weekend that I met him. I think you have to wait a week after your first missed period or something." My response was so inappropriate there was no doubting it was the truth. After I explained the urgency in contacting him (mostly to relieve my guilt, but also because I dug him), she took my number and promised to give it to her son. I heard from him twenty minutes later, to which began the six-month long-distance relationship. At that time, Skype was a mere vision, and Internet phone service was so horrendous, you were lucky if you could hear more than static and EVPs, so we racked up quite the long-distance bills, talking on the phone every night (which allowed me to uncover those Las Vegas white lies, one by one).

Two months later, when talking on the phone began to seem like a cheap substitute, I planned a weekend trip to San Diego. I was crazy about this guy. I had to see him, and I definitely had to have sex with him. I was happily going to break one of my own rules, which is to never have sex with a guy before three months of dating. It weeds out the weirdos that aren't worth the notch on your bed post, and honestly, it takes me that long to know whether I even like someone enough to get naked in front of them. It had only been two months, and I was uncharacteristically ready to throw Dave down and ravage him. As I had made that fact well known, he booked a hotel.

After getting a facial, massage, manicure, pedicure, and pep talk from Carrie the night before, I was ready for an adventure as my plane touched down in San Diego. It gets a little fuzzy after that. I don't even remember Dave picking me up at the airport. The only thing I remember about the entire trip was the ridiculous number of times we had sex in two days. Sex and eat. That's all we did. Oh, and an unfortunate and embarrassing incident regarding chewing gum. I'll spare you those details.

So began our trips back and forth to visit. We would take turns flying out to see each other every other month or so. I can recall the exact moment that I realized I was in love. I had known him for about four months, and I was sitting in an Auto Zone parking lot with Carrie. Suddenly I had a weird, topsy-turvy feeling invade my gut. I gasped, looked wide-eyed over at Carrie, and said, "I think I'm in love with Dave."

She laughed, put her sunglasses on, and while backing out of the spot, said, "Of course you are, dumbass. Are you seriously just figuring that out?" Yep. My middle name is *a day late and a dollar short*, remember?

Dave had been professing his love for me since day one, so he was relieved and really happy that night, when I told him the Auto Zone parking lot story. I had jumped on the love bandwagon, which put us in a whole new category. Phone calls and visits every other month were no longer going to cut it. One of us was going to have to move, and you don't have to be gifted to figure out who was going where. I made arrangements to move. I had eight weeks to find a job in San Diego. A month or so later, it was Dave's turn to visit me in Kansas. It was supposed to be the last visit either one of us would have to make, as I was scheduled to move to San Diego the following month. When I picked him up from the airport, he was acting weird; when we watched movies later that night, he was still acting weird; and when we woke up the next day, he was *still* acting weird. The girl that could normally do no wrong could do no right in his eyes. He was picking at me for everything, including my use of colorful language. I swear too much? Did he really say that? Something was up, and I was pretty sure it wasn't good.

Because my imagination is far worse than reality, I'm a communicator. I like to get it all on the table. I like to know facts. I don't want to have to guess, because as I said, what I imagine is almost always worse than the true situation. The quicker something is resolved, the quicker you move forward, and I like to keep moving forward at all times. Besides, it's less messy and more productive. With those qualities pushing me to get to the bottom of what was going on, I asked Dave if he wanted to go for a walk. He agreed. My apartment complex was located on a golf course, and we were walking along the cart path when Dave said suddenly, "I don't want you to move to San Diego." I stopped and looked at him. I could feel my mouth hanging open, and I couldn't even force myself to close it. My normally spot-on intuition had not seen this coming. I thought for sure it was going to have to do with my excessive drinking or marijuana smoking, as those are the only things he really nagged me about…and occasionally my language, if I was on a roll.

To a casual observer, I was waiting patiently for him to share the thoughts and feelings that led him to his current stand on our relationship, but I'll be honest. Inside, I was blown away. My gut was flipping around. I couldn't get it to stop, and it was making me nauseous. My heart was reverberating through my ears, and I could feel my hands shaking as they were clasped together (probably so I wouldn't sock him). My armpits felt the usual thousands of fire ants clamoring to have their way with me, and I had to force myself not to violently thrust my fingers under my arms and start tearing away at the delicate (and likely whiskery) skin with my unmanicured nails. I couldn't even hear what he was saying due to the freight train of thoughts that rushed my brain. It didn't take long for the internal panic to manifest externally. That's when the seventh hole witnessed a tirade that would have put Kanye to shame. Swearing, screaming, crying, stomping, sitting, spitting, standing, hopping on one foot, more swearing...you get the idea. All I could think about was that I had already quit my job, packed up most of my crap, gone through the immense torture of a garage sale, given notice to my apartment, and was getting ready to attend a going-away party that my friends were throwing me. For what? Turns out he really couldn't give me a reason other than he couldn't handle the pressure of me moving to San Diego for him. He didn't want to feel responsible for me or my happiness, and he thought I was giving my life up for him. *Evil laugh.* Silly boy. He didn't know me well enough to understand that the only path I like to follow is my own. Granted, it's crooked, rocky, and unpredictable, but it's *my* path, dammit.

He ended up flying home the next day, three days earlier than his original itinerary. I was in tears as we said good-bye, confused by his claim to still love me while at the same time not wanting my company. We didn't speak for four weeks. Those weeks were tough, as daily I went back and forth on which path to take. I was definitely moving away from Kansas. I had lived there for seventeen years, and I knew it was time to once again spread my wings. I had two options—the first being San Diego. I had some good job leads, and three interviews would be waiting for me when I got there. On top of that, it was San Diego. My heart belonged to California (Christa has called me "Hollywood" for years), and after conservative Kansas, I was ready to be back amongst the "fruits and nuts." The second option was Texas, near my mom and Bob. It was only six hours from Wichita, and if I wanted to, I would be able to stay with them until I found a job. Not as cool, but doable.

As it turns out, I didn't have to make that difficult decision. My horoscope made it for me. Let me rephrase that—my horoscope triggered something in my conscience that already knew the correct path, which allowed said horoscope to scream at me from under the "Aquarius" heading for June, "Move to San Diego, you freaking idiot!" It didn't really say that. I don't actually remember what it said, but it was quite obvious that the universe thought the San Diego path was the one to take, Dave or no Dave. I wasn't really worried about the whole Dave thing. I knew that would eventually work itself out one way or the other, and I wasn't invested in any certain outcome. Who was I to say which role he was playing? He could be my soul mate, or he could have just been the catalyst for the desperately needed changes I was making since he arrived in my life. I really didn't care either way. My mom always said, "If it's meant to be, it will happen. You still need to try 100 percent to get what you want, but after that, if it's meant to be, it will happen." Thank you, Mom. There is no mantra I use more in my everyday life. It adds peace to my chaos, and creates a handle for me to hold on to when I feel like I might be slipping. That being said, I had to break it to Dave that I was headed that way, and I was pretty sure he didn't have the same "change is fun" outlook on life that I did.

Chapter 15

I wouldn't be stretching it to say that an engagement lasting longer than twenty-four seconds would probably never end with the marriage and the baby carriage. My thought was, *Make it fifteen seconds*, just to be on the safe side.

My friend Barb and I planned our trip at the same time, as she was moving to Phoenix, which was on the way. We decided to do it together, and I packed everything I owned (other than the twelve boxes I shipped to San Diego via UPS) into my jeep, and we towed it behind Barb's U-Haul. My friends waved good-bye as we drove away, both to begin a new life. Barb was going to Phoenix to be closer to her kids. I didn't know what the fuck I was doing, but I was doing something, and that's all that mattered. I was beyond excited to see what the future held. I expected nothing less than greatness.

We were driving through beautiful, dusty New Mexico, when my cell phone rang for the hundredth time. Everyone dutifully called daily to make sure we hadn't run into any roadside stranglers or rapists. When I looked at the number, my stomach did a triple-twisted, quadruple backflip while my heart started beating ferociously. It was Dave calling. I hadn't seen this coming! Intuition,

0 for 3! He asked me where I was. I told him we were somewhere in the bowels of New Mexi— He didn't even let me finish before he told me that he had changed his mind, and he couldn't wait for me to get there, and we were going to have so much fun together, life was grand, blah, blah, blah, et cetera, et cetera, et cetera. Silly boy. He had no idea what he was talking about, and I knew it. I was pretty sure things would get worse and not better when I arrived, but I agreed to call him when I got into town. He said that his parents insisted that I stay with them, instead of a hotel, while I looked for a place to live, so I agreed. It was only three days later that I was moving the contents of my jeep into my new studio apartment, and Dave had already started acting weird again. We had spent the previous two days looking for apartments by the beach to no avail. There was a waiting list for those that were in my price range, and I didn't have time to wait.

The only place that I could get into happened to be right by Dave's house (thankfully, he was with me on the entire apartment adventure, and knew that to be the case, so it didn't look like I was stalking him). I wasn't sure if that's what triggered his freak-out, but I knew his freak-out when I saw it, and this time, I was not going to be a willing participant. After going to lunch with his mom, with her advice to dump him confirming my gut feeling to do the same, I did just that. Again, whatever's meant to be…If you love something, set it free…you get the picture. It only took two weeks before he called me to let me know that he was finally ready to love me. Ready to love me? The weird thing is, he's not the first guy that has ever said that to me, and I often wonder why a person would feel the need to *prepare* themselves to love me. Like a fighter jumping around the box, seconds away from the first punch trying to psych himself up. What does that say about me? It can't be good.

To my shock and delight, the next five or six months were pretty much perfect. Surprisingly Dave had kept his word and hadn't had another freak out. He and I had found our groove, and I was working at the ad agency. Because of my instant connection with my co-workers, I had found my own friends and social scene immediately, which I think took some of the pressure off of our relationship. We even planned to ask for furniture that Christmas, with the intention of Dave moving in to my apartment, when he could get the guts to tell his parents.

Dave's parents took it as well as could be expected, with their son wanting to cohabitate, out of wedlock, with a girl he met in Las Vegas. It turns out, they were praying for our sins every night for no reason at all (or their prayers actually worked), because a week after Dave moved in, he moved right back out. Yep…another freaking freak-out. *Come on*! Five days into it, he started acting weird. Two days later, I asked him if he wanted to move out, because he was acting like a weirdo. He said yes, he did want to move out. He *was* freaking out, but he was worried that I would be mad or hurt. I was pretty much the opposite of mad or hurt. I actually laughed, and thought to myself, "This ain't my first rodeo with you, mister." By then, I knew the dance, and I knew how to keep us two-stepping after a stumble. I told him, no problem, we could go back to how we were a week ago. We'll act like he never moved in. We won't even tell anyone. He was clearly relieved, and I just thought it was the funniest story ever, destined to go in my "book" that seemed to write itself as I plodded along through life. He moved out that same day.

You might be asking yourself how either one of us, with our personal relationship dysfunctions, ever managed to make it to the altar. Good question! Though I love the ones I love, I am a terrible commitment-phobe. Relationships are hard enough, but marriage is a different beast that I wasn't sure I would ever be able to manage, and as Christa's husband, Darren, so poignantly brought to my attention during my going away party; I was only averaging about two years per relationship before I would hit the road, and two years a successful marriage does not make. I would have told him to shut his face, but we've known each other for a long time, and he's been privy to all of my adventures, so I had to respect his logic. Also, if I want to be entirely honest, I wasn't sure what I thought of the whole marriage thing, anyway. First of all, nothing pisses me off more than doing something because it's "what you're supposed to do." I'll question *supposed-to-dos* and *shoulds* every time, and if they don't resonate with me, I'll dump them. As the saying goes, "Don't *should* on yourself, and don't let others *should* on you, either!" As far as relationships go, I see a bigger picture than that piece of paper filed at the courthouse. I see souls connected to souls for reasons much more complicated than what our human brains can even imagine. There's a poem out there called "Reason, Season, Lifetime," which basically says that different people come into our lives for…wait for it…wait for it…a reason, a season, or a lifetime. I wanted to include it, but there's a big scuffle going on about whom the true author is, so you'll just have to look it up. My point is: who are we to decide which category someone falls into? I could have every intention of staying with one person for the rest of my life (and I do), but it doesn't necessarily mean it's going to happen. What if I stick them in the "lifetime" category, and they should have been in the "season" category? Marriage, friendship, or relationship, I'll tell you what happens: a sense of failure. Two people wrongly believing they have failed because they couldn't make it work for a lifetime, when unbeknownst to them, a single season was the plan all along. They don't realize they should be happy to have experienced it rather than be sad that it has ended! Who needs the unnecessary pressure? With that being said, I want to make it clear that just because I believe in the method behind the madness of people coming in and out our lives for different reasons, it doesn't mean we should take a laissez-faire attitude toward maintaining the relationships we currently have, because that can screw it up before we've gleaned everything from them we were meant to learn, which would equally suck, in my book. I also want to make it clear that though I think marriage can be unnecessary, I think everyone should be allowed to experience the lesson of marriage if it's something they want to do. Seriously, in the grand scheme of things, who the heck are we to dictate who should and shouldn't connect? That's a sore subject for me…I once told Dave we should get divorced and not remarry until it was legal for all humans. He rolled his eyes and shook his head, but I think he must have felt bad, because later that night, he was dead serious when he told me that we could call ourselves *life partners* instead of *husband and wife*, if it would make me feel better about marriage inequality. I almost peed myself trying not to laugh, and gently rejected his offer.

As is always the case, there's a massive amount of thought generated to form my opinions, and from my thoughts above, you can understand why

I probably wasn't the best candidate for marriage. Between that and Dave's tendency to run scared at every fork in the relationship road, I wouldn't be stretching it to say that an engagement lasting longer than twenty-four seconds would probably never end with the marriage and the baby carriage. My thought was, *Make it fifteen seconds*, just to be on the safe side. Don't give me time to analyze it.

Peace Out Toto!

This was at my going away party. Either everyone was happy to see me go or Christa made her margaritas.

(clockwise, l to r) Christa, Carrie, me, Donya & Jennifer

Chapter 16

Oh, great, look what that whore from Kansas is doing to our son now....

It was March of 2001. Three months had passed since Dave had moved out, but due to my badass two-stepping skills, and Dave's new understanding and respect of the importance of communication, we never missed a beat. Life was good, and we were in love. I fully expected another freak-out at some point, but I wasn't worried about it. I came to look at those freak-outs as visible proof that Dave was growing and changing inside as a person by leaps and bounds, and let's face it, growth and change for a human is not comfortable on any scale. I got it, and explained it to him, so he got it. So with my permission to freak out when necessary, it became less necessary for him to freak out. Isn't it stupid how that works?

I was driving to work one morning, when I heard an ad on the radio. They were casting for a show called *Surprise Wedding II* on FOX, and after hearing the premise, I was shocked there was ever a *Surprise Wedding I*. They were looking for women who were willing to surprise their boyfriends by asking *them* for *their* hand in marriage on national TV...basically putting them on the spot, and hoping for the best. "Oh, my God! Who would ever do that?" I couldn't imagine having the balls those girls would need, and cringed for their poor boyfriends who would be losing theirs.

I didn't think much else about it as I drove through downtown, watching the harbor blinking in the morning sun. Not because it wasn't a fascinating and uncomfortable idea, but because living in San Diego, I was at most times presented with a magnificent view of the Pacific Ocean, whose overwhelming presence had a tendency to keep me present, and my active mind out to lunch...you know, "Back in One Hour. Please Call Again."

At work, I wasn't able to even lay my things down in my office before my friend Jen came rushing in with a shit-eating grin permeating her face. I was immediately nervous. "What?" I thought for sure I had screwed something up.

She giggled in a sort of evil way and then asked me if I had heard the *Surprise Wedding II* casting call spot on the radio when I was driving to work. Because of a mysterious twinkle in her eye, I was afraid to admit that I had, but I finally erupted with, "Yes! Who in their right mind would *ever* do that? I would absolutely *die* of embarrassment!"

She quickly responded with "You! You have to! You guys have the coolest story! Call them! Now! Now! They would pay for your dress, your ring, and your honeymoon! Come on!" It took more arguing than that, but in the end, Jen is from New York, and her accent alone scared me into making that call. I dialed the 1-800 number that she had so graciously copied down, and very anticlimactic-like, left a message with my name, brief story of my relationship, and phone number, in case I sounded interesting. As our days at work mostly consisted of putting out fires, once we started working that morning, we pretty much forgot about the crazy TV show phone call. Most of my time at work was spent on the phone, answering it or returning calls. In a lot of cases, I was either getting yelled at or yelling at someone else. As you can imagine, if I ever had to leave the office for any reason, I dreaded listening to all of the messages that blinked angrily at me through the lone red light on my phone when I returned. Sometimes I would have to psych myself up for a couple of hours before I was able to listen to the messages, knowing it would be a long list of people wanting things from me. Ugh.

That afternoon was no different, as I jabbed my index fingers in my eyes listening to the messages that had accumulated during my lunch break. I was genuinely shocked to hear a message from a lady named Marki introducing herself as the casting director for the FOX project, *Surprise Wedding II.* She stated that I sounded interesting and gave me a direct number to reach her so she could learn more about me. Holy shit! I yelled for Jen to hurry to my office, but that probably wasn't the best way to get her attention. We had open-topped offices, and every one of us used the same form of communication throughout the office: yelling. We would yell questions and answers back and forth to each other all day.

Me: HEY KATHLEEN?

Kathleen: WHAT?

Me: HOW MUCH ARE THOSE STUPID MINIATURE TOOL SETS WE'RE USING FOR THE GIVEAWAY?

Kathleen: WE AREN'T USING TOOLSETS FOR THE GIVEAWAY; WE'RE USING WEATHER RADIOS!

Me: OH, SHIT. ARE YOU SURE? SHIT! I ORDERED THE STUPID MINIATURE TOOLSETS!

(Stifled giggles floating from the top of every office.)

Jen showed up a couple of minutes later, and I immediately played the voicemail for her. She laughed and laughed and then, still laughing, forced me to agree to return Marki's call. I went into a conference room for the call of shame, so as not to be the office entertainment that afternoon. Marki answered before I had a chance to lose my courage. She was really fun on the phone and loved my story. She invited me to audition in person at her office in L.A., which I agreed to without hesitation. After writing down the details, I hung up the phone and let the freak out begin. An audition in front of Marki was scary enough, but before we said our good-byes, she informed me that I would also be auditioning in front of the *Extra* and *Entertainment Tonight* cameras, which made the whole thing a bit more real. It wasn't just the TV show; it was the possibility of getting married as a result of the TV show. I really needed to think about whether or not marriage would turn out to be the best decision for me and Dave. Though the idea of doing the show sounded really fun, I wasn't about to wreck my life for my fifteen minutes of fame! I had some serious ruminating to do.

As my thoughts turned over that night, I began to entertain the idea of being married to Dave. I felt pretty conflicted, because my logical side was telling me that Dave was too young (he was still in college), and marriage would be an unnecessary commitment. Unfortunately (or fortunately), my intuition was in disagreement, screaming at me that this was the path I was supposed to follow. I was used to the left and right side of my brain arguing. It happens daily as a result of me being part of the five percent or so of the population that equally uses both sides of the brain. It causes difficulty for me sometimes, because I see and understand both sides of an issue, logically and emotionally, so it's hard to come to any conclusions. After spinning around in the gerbil wheel of my mind for a few hours, I finally came to the conclusion that I couldn't come to a conclusion. The next morning, I called my mom to get some help from the other side, meaning the sane and normal side. I knew I needed the opinion of someone that wasn't just looking out for *me*. I needed someone that was looking out for me, Dave, and our relationship. My mom is a logistics engineer by trade, and has an incredibly logical mind, which is balanced out beautifully by her intuition and keen understanding of universal laws. She is quite possibly the most balanced and sane person I have ever met.

In a nutshell, she was horrified yet curious by the idea of the TV show. She said *she* would never do it, but that's kind of an inside joke because she would never do *any* of the things I'm usually up for. After getting over the shock of the premise of the show and that I was even entertaining the thought of it, we got down to the meat of the issue. Would it be for the highest good of everyone involved if Dave and I were to marry? She asked me what my gut said. I told her my gut said to do it…or at least to try. After mulling over things for a bit, we decided the best thing to do would be to implement the "give it 100 percent" plan, meaning, go through all of the motions, do my best, and if it was meant to be, it would happen. I felt happy with that. I had faith that everything would work out no matter what, but I also wanted to get Dave's parents' take on the situation, just in case the universe decided that marriage was our path. I wasn't sure how they would respond.

You'd think they would have been like, "Oh great, look what that whore from Kansas is doing to our son now," but they weren't like that at all! They were actually really excited about the idea…so excited even that Dave's dad offered to drive me into L.A. for the audition, which was scheduled for the following day. I had mixed emotions about his offer. On one hand, I could look for the address without trying to drive at the same time, but on the other hand, I knew I would need that two-and-a-half hour car ride to flip-the-fuck-out, and I didn't particularly want to do that in the presence of Dave's dad, as he was practically driving me to the church to marry his son.

I finally agreed. The car ride was uneventful, and I was calmer than I thought I would be. Thanks to my TV background, I wasn't nervous about the audition, and I had put marriage into the hands of the universe, so the only thing I saw in my near future was an adventure. I didn't even care if I didn't make it past the audition. Just doing the audition was going to be an experience, and I am a true collector of life experiences. I live for life experiences. I put them in my pocket like shiny rocks, and take them out every now and then to appreciate and reflect on them. I once read an article that the Eastern Indian culture considers those with AD(H)D to be old, wise souls that are coming to the end of their reincarnations, so they must pack as many life experiences and lessons into their few remaining lifetimes as possible. Makes sense to me—that's why we always have so much shit going on!

Marki's waiting room was cramped when I found my way in. There were only about three or four other girls, but one brought her mom (Dave's dad elected to wait in the car, thank God), and we all had scrapbooks full of proof of our love, as requested by Marki. In other words, they needed to see if the guy was presentable enough to throw on TV. The girl that had her mom with her was particularly chatty, and asked to see everyone's scrapbooks, which totally freaked me out. Of course, by the time she asked me, everyone else had agreed, and I didn't want to look like an asshole, so I let her look through it. She kept going on and on about how we were soooooo cute, and we would toooooootally be on the show. She was really nice, just a bit overbearing for my taste. Her name was Wendy and she was a limo driver. Soon after that, I was called into the back room where the *Extra* and *Entertainment Tonight* cameras waited. I told Wendy good-bye, never thinking that I would run into her again.

The calm I had been feeling suddenly dropped away as I entered the studio. There were three cameras facing a lone chair, with another chair next to the cameras. Marki walked up to me and introduced herself. She was really bubbly and hyper, which for some reason triggered the bubbly and hyper in me…times ten. She told me to sit in the lonely chair, and she sat across from me. The cameras now had operators, and my audition was about to begin.

I was a F-R-E-A-K. I can't describe it any other way. I was so insanely hyper, that I never shut the hell up the entire audition. I was so animated, I'm not sure how I even stayed in my chair. I was so in the moment that I couldn't control my language, and then honestly pondered out loud whether or not I might be suffering from Tourette's syndrome. Marki laughed and laughed and laughed, and I was a force to be reckoned with. It was surreal. It felt like I was performing stand-up and she just kept laughing, fueling my performance. It was a really cool experience, and strange but satisfying to see a different part of me. I thought I knew me so well! It's funny because we call my son Nikko "Baby Eddie," as in Eddie Murphy, because of his inclination toward performing daily stand-up routines, and his uncanny ability to implement a potty word into any conversation without making it obvious.

Here's a perfect example; the other day I overheard the kids talking as they were looking through a photo album.

Willow: Were you still in Mom's tummy in this picture?

Nikko: No, it was before that...I think I was still in Dad's wiener.

Baby Eddie! He gets really pissed when we call him Baby Eddie, which makes it even funnier. I guess he comes by it honestly, as his dad is just like him, and that particular day in the audition, I was "Mama Eddie."

After my audition was over, Marki told me I was just the type of girl FOX was looking for, and that she was going to send my information to the producers. She explained that she was sending a gaggle of girls for them to look through, and in the end it was their choice. She wished me luck and sent me on my way.

I have no idea how long it was before I got a call. It could have been two days; it could have been two weeks; I have no idea, but I got the call, and that's all that mattered. A lady named Sally Ann was on the other end of the line when I picked up the phone that day. What a nice surprise, considering I thought it was going to be one of my clients yelling at me again. Sally Ann was a producer for *Surprise Wedding II*, and I immediately loved her. She sounded exactly like my friend Jen from work. They had the same accent and the same "don't hold back" attitude. I love it when people say what they think. You don't have to guess at anything, and it leaves no room for miscommunication. They also had the same dry sense of humor, which is one of my favorites. Dry humor keeps me on my toes...are they serious or joking? Serious or joking? Serious or joking? Later on, I found out that they were both from Long Island, which explained some of the similarities.

That immediate comfort with Sally Ann allowed me to roll through the forty-five-minute phone interview with ease. She asked me tons of questions about myself, Dave, and the two of us together. She loved the fact that Dave had moved out after living with me for one week, and when I was telling her the story, I had no idea it would end up being my story, down the road. At the end of the call, and after answering all of her questions, she told me she was going to have another producer, Billy, call me the next day. She wanted to get his opinion on me as well. I told her that was great, and promised to be myself per her request. I loved that she said that to me. My whole life, people have been telling me not to be myself, and she was telling me that my success was riding on being the person I actually was. It gave me an enormous, and much needed, amount of relief that I wouldn't have to keep myself reigned in. Being myself comes much more naturally to me. Isn't that a ridiculous statement? You would think that would be common sense, but it isn't! Look at all of the people in the world either asking someone else to change or trying to change for someone else. It's absurd! I'm not talking about self-improvement plans here, people. We all have areas that need improvement, and sometimes another person has to point them out. What I'm saying is that we can't change who our basic being is. We were made the way we were made for a reason. We don't always know what that reason is, and that's where you have to have faith—the ability to believe in something you can't see. And still today, I'm not entirely sure why I was given this brain. On bad days, I cry and cuss at this brain that gives me so much heartache, and as much as I want to hate it, and as I'm calling it vile names, and pounding my head on the bed to punish it, I can't. I can't hate it, because I love it so much, and that just makes me cry harder. YOU CRAP-ASS BRAIN…SHIT! CAN'T YOU JUST FREAKING HELP ME OUT A LITTLE HERE? I KNOW YOU'RE TRYING YOUR BEST, AND I APPRECIATE THAT BECAUSE I DO LOVE YOU, BUT I HAVE TO BE HONEST HERE, YOU'RE FUCKING KILLING ME. BUT STILL, I WOULDN'T TRADE YOU FOR THE WORLD! (Sob.)

Billy called the next day. He was equally awesome, and by the end of the call, I had a pretty good idea that they liked me, but as I was just about to find out, there were many more hoops ahead that needed to be jumped, and one in particular was a burning hoop. I had never really *sincerely* questioned my sanity until the day I had to speak on the phone to a psychologist provided by FOX. It was a mandatory, thirty-minute phone call where he was to determine my level of crazy. He was basically trying to ascertain how I would act in the event Dave rejected my proposal. Would I kill Dave? Would I kill myself? Have I killed anyone else? I was nervous all day before that interview. What if I really was crazy? It's not like I would know if I were crazy, so it was a perfectly acceptable idea that I could be, and just have no idea! It turns out, either I'm not crazy, or I fooled the doctor, because after two separate interviews with him, and passing the thirty-five-page background check where they called some of my ex-boyfriends just to make sure I wasn't lying about killing one of them, I had made it to the final round. Finally, the producers had to pass their choices off to the FOX executives who would be making the final decision. By that time, I had gotten to know Sally Ann and Billy pretty well. I knew they were rooting for me, and I just kept telling myself, *if it's meant to happen, it will.* They told me they really wanted me to be on the show, and promised to be in touch as soon as they heard something.

It may have been a week later that Sally Ann called me at work. Unfortunately, the call was to let me know that they didn't know anything yet, and were still waiting to hear back from FOX. Apparently, there were thousands of audition tapes that were mailed in, and they had to be considered as well. I think it was only a couple of days after that that I received the "actual" call from Sally Ann telling me that I had made the show. In the next breath, she informed me that I had three days to feed Dave a bogus story, wrap everything up at work, and jump on a plane headed to Las Vegas, the city where it had all begun.

The producers came up with a cover story for each of the seven girls that had made the show, and Fed Ex-ed us the material to back up our stories. My story for Dave was that I entered a "Love, Las Vegas Style" contest for a magazine, where I wrote in and recounted the humorous tale of our initial encounter in Las Vegas. *If only that were the case,* says my lazy self, *then I could just copy and paste from that, instead of having to write it all down for this book!* I really am that lazy, too. I have to argue with that lazy self every day, just to get things done—it's insane. Anyway, the point is, Dave believed the story. They were getting him to Vegas by paying for his expenses to fly out, stay in a hotel, gamble, and watch me receive the "award." I think that softened the blow of me randomly blowing town for ten days to do GodknowswhatItoldhim. He wanted to see the article I had written to win, and I had to tell him that I sent the magazine my master copy, as those were the rules…there could be no copies except the one submitted to the magazine. "You didn't save even *one* copy for yourself or your records?"

"No. Those were the rules! I know! I thought it was stupid, too, but come on! I won!" He turned his head, squinted his eyes, and looked at me as if I were the dumbest person he had ever laid eyes on, and I'm telling you, I didn't blame him one bit! I was embarrassed that he even *thought* I was that stupid, but my dumb ass wasn't about to try to write an article to prove my intelligence! Again, I was so lazy, I preferred he think of me as a complete idiot than to put forth the effort it would take to write out a fake story.

A couple of days later, I was at the airport, trying to figure out how to get to Vegas, as I had missed my plane. I wasn't late getting to the airport, as one might imagine. Instead, I thought my flight was at an entirely different time than it actually was. How that might have happened, I have no idea. I've just come to expect those hiccups, so I happily boarded the next flight, excited for the adventure ahead. After I landed, I made my way through the airport, where I finally saw a guy standing with a sign that said "Fundaburk." There aren't many with that last name, so I assumed it was for me.

Just last week, I asked Willow, "Do you know that my name used to be Fundaburk?"

She just looked at me, wrinkled her nose, and said, "Gosh…I'm glad you changed it to *Stacey*." That's my kid!

The guy was from the show, and there was a cute blonde standing next to him that he had already wrangled from another flight. Her name was Tammy, and she was also one of the brides-to-maybe. We were escorted to a limo and climbed inside, giggling. After yelling out the window, we did the cliché standing through the sunroof, whooping and hollering as we made our way toward the strip. As you know, I'm a big fan of experiences, and I had a pretty good idea the next ten days were going to be chock-full of them.

We were shown to Sally Ann's hotel room, which was used as a sort of holding room for the girls to wait until the others arrived. When Tammy and I walked in, there were already two girls waiting in the room. Their names were Lauren and Deidra, and I knew immediately that I was going to like them. Deidra was sweet and young, and Lauren had the mouth of a trucker with the swagger of a prom queen. The remaining three filtered in over the next hour, with a knock at the door announcing another ingredient to be added to the crazy stew that was our life at that moment. Eva was a knockout—a blonde, blue-eyed girl from Alaska with big boobs and a super-toned physique. Michelle was definitely the most timid when she came in. She later told us that she felt like she didn't really fit in when she saw the rest of us, which was nuts, but I think it's mostly because she wasn't sure how this whole thing was going to turn out for her and her hockey-player boyfriend.

Later that week when we were trying on wedding dresses, Michelle starting tearing up when she looked at herself in the mirror wearing her new, white gown. She said she had a dream the night before that during the show, she was the only girl turned down by her prospective groom. For one second, I wondered if it was her intuition or just nerves, but then forgot all about it, as I do most things that briefly touch my mind.

Chapter 17

I think she may have even started keeping bacon in her pockets so she could make it through her taping without cursing.

When a knock at the door announced the arrival of the final girl, you can imagine my complete and utter shock when in waltzes Wendy, the girl from the waiting room at the audition. Remember—the one that violated me by asking to see my scrapbook? I couldn't believe it. She seemed so overbearing and obnoxious at the audition. It's not like she wasn't friendly...I mean, in *my* book, she was way too friendly, but we just have to keep in mind that I'm slow to warm up. She just seemed like such a strange choice. It wasn't long before everyone understood why Wendy was chosen. She was the token "loose cannon."

We were together nonstop for those ten days, most of which, for me, were all blurred together. Our time was spent rehearsing, taping excursions (picking out our dresses, etc.), doing solo interviews, writing our lines, and eating. We also "worked out." My workout consisted of me getting on a treadmill for five minutes and then wandering out to the nickel slots so conveniently located next to the gym entrance. One time I won a hundred dollars on one nickel. *One* nickel! Anyone that plays nickel slots knows you have to play the max amount of nickels per pull to get anything worthwhile back! Can you imagine how much I would have won had I done that? The security guard that responded to the flashing lights and siren of my Betty Boop Devil slot-machine was sure to tell me what an idiot I was for only playing one nickel. I was more concerned that I had snuck out of the gym and was currently the center of attention for hitting a major "jackpot." Somehow I managed through that situation unnoticed and was able to gracefully make my way back into the gym to get back on the treadmill for five minutes before we all headed back to our rooms.

It was a pretty grueling schedule, and most days we started early in the morning, continuing into the evening. The only time we were ever alone was when we were in our hotel rooms, going down for the night. The show, thankfully and thoughtfully, had given us our own rooms, which was really important to me, because I cannot live without alone time. My sanity depends on it. With all that in mind, it's still surprising to me that I ended up spending only one night alone. Eva and I had an instant and very strong connection. I had a connection with almost all of the girls, but the connection with Eva was more intense, and frankly we wanted to maximize every minute we were going to have together, so beginning on night two, we took turns sleeping in either my room or hers, just talking and talking and talking about everything and anything. She even taught me a new word. I can't think of it now, but I always know it when I hear it. It was so strange, because normally, as an introvert, I need alone time to re-energize, but with Eva, she didn't take energy from me, she gave me energy, yet being with her was as calming to me as my alone time. It was so cool. I felt like I had known her forever, and we talked as the sun came up on more than one occasion. We soon noticed, however, how the lack of sleep was affecting our bodies, so we vowed to make ourselves stop talking at a certain hour. We didn't want to look ghastly for the show, so we followed that bedtime rule, and it all worked smashingly.

I'm not gonna lie—we also spent a lot of time eating. Imagine if you had full access to the hotel's basement employee cafeteria, twenty-four hours a day—an enormous buffet, with anything you could ever dream of…for free. Can you imagine being able to eat whatever you want, whenever you want to? Sure, you wouldn't want to do that forever, but for a week or so it wouldn't be terrible. As you can imagine, it wasn't terrible. One night Sally and the others took us to a really nice restaurant on the strip. They felt bad that we were stuck inside so much. It was lovely, and the food was delicious, but in the end, we all agreed we would have rather been in the basement cafeteria under our hotel, which Lauren lovingly referred to as "the world's most delicious restaurant," so she could eat the bacon that magically made her less grumpy. It's true; I saw it with my own eyes. I think she may have even started keeping bacon in her pockets so she could make it through her taping without cursing. Taping our solo interviews was also *my* least-favorite thing to do. I was encouraged to let some tears roll during taping, where on a normal day, unless I was PMS-ing, I wouldn't even consider. I also had to answer questions about my relationship with Dave and then get coached on how to give the same answer in a different way to maximize time for the show. That required instant memorizing, which is impossible for me, especially when I'm being told verbally. As you can imagine, I had many takes, so it made me feel crappy. I didn't find out until later that all of the other girls had the same experience, and I finally gave myself a break.

It was during one of those interviews that I began to see a pattern in the questions and figured out that we all had a "story." My story was that Dave had moved in with me and moved out a week later, which didn't make his parents happy when they watched the show. Eva's story was that she had met her boyfriend only a week after his divorce. Lauren met her guy on the Internet. Deidra was with her high school sweetheart. Michelle's boyfriend was against marriage (you can see why she was nervous). Wendy's story was that her brother had heart disease and his dying wish was for her to get married. I don't remember Tammy's story. They apparently had to cut a lot of footage when they edited the show and unfortunately Tammy didn't make it through the editing. I felt bad for her when I found out. All of that craziness for nothing…though the best part of the deal ended up being the experience, and not the final product, so I would like to think Tammy was OK with how it all turned out. Anyway, I really didn't like my "story," but when I brought it up, I had to agree with Sally that it would make for better TV, even if I looked like a complete dumbass.

There were parts of the show that were taped outside of our hotel. Those were our little excursions. On one hand, our excursions were great because we got to breathe fresh air by leaving the hotel. On the other hand, the cameras were on us every second, so we couldn't really let loose and be free. One time we were shooting some b-roll by a fountain outside our hotel, and in true Wendy fashion, she shot her arm into the fountain, and wildly brought up her cupped hand, drenching us as we posed pretty while the camera rolled. Lauren almost kicked her ass for that one, though Wendy did a million things like that a day. She basically didn't have a good grasp of boundaries, so she annoyed the shit out of everyone, she knew she annoyed the shit out of everyone, and she loved annoying the shit out of every one. My favorite story of the whole trip involves a stand-off between Wendy and Lauren after one of our writing sessions. To set it up right, we were required to write our own lines for the show, so Sally would gather us in her room, and we would all spend hours writing the different lines for the different segments. When we finished, we would show them to her, and she would guide us on which changes to make, or approve them. It was tough being stuck in that room for that long, and most of us didn't like writing our lines, so things could get a bit tense. The fact that almost all of us had strong personalities (producers included) didn't help. It was, however, what added the texture and colors to the experience, so I would have never wanted it any other way, but in a tense environment, things can get a bit rocky.

We were all sitting around, mentally exhausted, when Wendy suddenly jumped to her feet and started bellowing, "Lauren! You fucking farted! You are so fucking disgusting…you're like a fucking man!" As soon as those words left her mouth, we all smelled the equivalent of a rotten egg, as the odor settled heavily around us like a fog. I lost it. I violently threw myself backward to express the enormous fit of laughter that erupted from me. Massive belly laughs were going off left and right. The smell and the accusation were too much to bear for our tired brains. Lauren, however, didn't find it quite as funny as the rest of us. She was up and in Wendy's face before I could even take a breath. They squared off chest to chest, doing the shoulder push, and were yelling in each other's faces. Lauren was screaming at Wendy that if she *had* farted she would have bragged about it. I think the word *bitch* may have been thrown around a few times before someone broke it up. I just remember thinking, if only people knew what happened behind the scenes of these shows. Here we have two blushing brides fighting over who farted. It took me a couple of hours (I'm pretty sure that's how long I laughed) before I could admit to the room that I was the phantom farter. It wasn't that I was trying to hide it, things just escalated so fast, I didn't have a chance to get a word in edge-wise, and by the end of it, I was laughing so hard, I couldn't even speak. Even days later, I would burst out laughing whenever I thought about it. You'll be happy to know that I eventually apologized for the backlash created by my horrendous fart, and named the consistent in-take of "the world's most delicious restaurant" as the culprit.

My second favorite memory is going to the jewelry store to see our "custom" rings. Apparently the jeweler that designed our rings also designed the ring for the show, *Who Wants to Marry a Millionaire*. My first thought was, "And we all know how that turned out." We knew our rings would probably be platinum, because we had to fill out a sheet for the show describing the type and style of ring we wanted, and we all wrote down that we wanted platinum. Worst-case scenario, we would take white gold—even sterling silver, as long as it wasn't yellow gold. Everyone wanted a big diamond, but would settle for a band as long as it was *platinum*. The cameras were on us as we all filed into the store, and settled around a large jewelry counter. This is what we had all been waiting for. Sally had kept the whole ring thing a surprise, and we were more than halfway through the ten days. The suave "custom jewelry designer" dramatically swept his hands under the counter and brought out a tray covered in black velvet. We all oohed and ahed for the camera. Lauren told him to "hurry up already." He gracefully peeled back the velvet cover to reveal seven shiny rings. There were more gasps, and then shock, as our eyes settled on the rings. Lauren and Deidra immediately begin to cry. I, of course, got the giggles. It was a pretty amazing sight. These rings were quite possibly the ugliest rings to have ever graced the face of this beautiful planet. They were so ugly that Lauren and Deidra were *crying from the ugliness.* Eva and I elbowed each other to keep from laughing at the jeweler that was obviously so proud of his work, he misinterpreted the crying for tears of *joy.* He smiled, with his black-dyed hair and hyper-white veneers reflecting the lights from the cameras. Not only was it *not* platinum, white gold, or sterling silver, it *was* yellow gold, and looked like something a romantic pimp might wear, if there ever were such a thing. The entire ring was textured like a gold nugget with a smoother area that ran around the middle. In that smooth area, there were *x*'s and *o*'s carved out in white gold, and they followed each other around the entire ring except for the back. The obvious "back" had a smooth area that ran vertically with no nugget texture or *x*'s and *o*'s. I'm assuming that was the extra left on for sizing purposes. To make matters worse (yet wickedly funny), teeny, tiny diamond chips were mounted in the middle of each "o." It was pretty tacky. I don't know how they even got any good footage out of that excursion. It went from bad to worse, as Lauren and Deidre were later pulled aside and talked to by Sally Ann about seeming "ungrateful," but I think Sally was as surprised by the "customness" of the rings as we were.

I don't remember a lot about the day we chose our gowns. We went into the store, and each had a clerk helping us search for our "perfect dress," assuming, of course, that our "perfect dress" happened to be one that was carried at a David's Bridal, which—surprise, surprise—mine wasn't. It was, however, *free*, so you won't hear me complaining. The only thing that really stands out for me is Michelle talking about her dream from the night before, worrying that she would be the only girl left at the altar, and my and Eva's behavior in front of the *Entertainment Tonight* cameras, who had a constant presence no matter where we went. It was getting late in the game, and we were over the novelty of cameras constantly in our faces, so we decided to do the worst interviews ever. We told the camera guy all about the "fart fight," and then began making up stories that involved things like us "catching the hotel bed on fire" and whatever else we could think of that couldn't possibly be used on air. Looking back, we probably acted like assholes, but I was sick of being "on," and the constant presence of the camera insisted on it. I don't know how "stars" (I use the term loosely in some cases) can function as normal people with paparazzi in their grill every time they step out of the house. I would go mad! I would be the person that shows up in the tabloids, a close-up shot of my anger-induced, disfigured face moments before I kick the pap in the nuts, and stomp on his fifteen-thousand-dollar camera. Needless to say, Eva and I didn't have a big part in the dress segment that aired.

Two or three days before we were to begin taping the actual show, the guys were ferried in under the false pretense of whatever bullshit story Sally Ann fed them. Dave came *this* close to not making it, on account of me supposedly "acting like a freak every time we talked on the phone." He said I acted like such a weirdo on the phone, he didn't even want to accept a free trip to Vegas. Well, yeah, I acted like a weirdo! This shit was so top-secret, we had to have a producer stand next to us and listen to any phone calls we made. It was so top-secret, the guys stayed at a different hotel, and were told they wouldn't see us for a couple of days, but were given food credits and gambling money, so they never made a peep about it. It was so top-secret, after the boys arrived in town, all of us girls had to pile into Sally Ann's room to sleep, which brings me to another Wendy story, bless her pea-pickin' heart.

We were all pretty excited when we knew the boys had landed. We got updates via producers that were hanging out with them, so we knew they were having a good time. Now, Wendy really wanted to see her man, I mean, *really wanted to see her man*. I'm too much of a prude to repeat what she said to all of us exactly, but you catch my drift. Anyway, as Wendy seemed to do with everything else, she took it to another level. That girl's impulsivity made me look like a bump on a log! Her great idea was to sneak out of the room and try to go find the guys at their hotel. As you can tell from above how much effort the producers put in to keeping us apart, none of us thought that was a very good idea. Don't get me wrong—I'm all about adventures, but the biggest reason I didn't think it was a great idea is because I wasn't willing to face the wrath of Sally if we got busted, and I'm pretty sure with Wendy leading the circus that would have been imminent. We told Wendy it wasn't going to happen, and she claimed she would just go by herself. As was the best course of action when dealing with Wendy in this state, we ignored her. It didn't work. Arguing between Lauren and Wendy ensued. Still didn't work. Wendy was determined to sneak out. This went on for the rest of the evening, until everyone finally went to bed. Wendy in Sally's bedroom, and the rest of us in the living room. Even in separate rooms, she continued to tell us of her "devious" plan, until finally, a couple of the girls got up and rigged a pile we called the *soda can alarm* inside both doors to our room, so we were finally able to relax and fall asleep. A couple of hours later, we all jumped up as a collision of cans broke the silence. The Alarm! To our surprise it wasn't Wendy. It was just Sally coming in. Why we didn't think of that part of the "alarm plan," I have no idea. She just said, "What the fuck?" stepped over the cans, and went into her room, kind of like, *that shit happens every day*. Wendy never made it out, due to falling asleep on the bed with her "club clothes" still on and still shiny.

OK, as I was saying before I got sidetracked, Dave almost didn't make the trip because of my phone mannerisms. I knew I was acting like a freak on the phone, but I didn't know how to act with someone standing next to me listening. I was afraid I would slip or say something wrong, so I just gave one-word answers to his questions. Not one of the conversations between Dave and I were normal. Not a one! When he told me he wasn't coming, I was already brain dead, so I just said, "I'll call you right back", hung up on him, and looked at the producer in panic! "He said he's not coming because I'm acting like a freak when I talk to him on the phone! I *told* you I was acting like a freak…now what?"

Sally came to the rescue, called Dave, and told him that there was nothing weird going on, and that he had to fly out because he was presenting me with an award, and then explained that I didn't know it yet, but I had won the entire "contest." Apparently that worked, because he showed up in Vegas when he was supposed to. I was glad I didn't have to talk to him those last three days we were in seclusion, because he probably would have flown directly home.

The last days were filled with rehearsals on the set. We practiced our lines that we had written, and figured out where to walk, stand, and look. That was fun for me. I had really missed being in front of the camera, and felt completely at ease with the idea of millions of viewers. It was the live people that I was worried about. There was going to be more than two thousand people in the studio audience! That could be weird. The only other issue that was bothering me was something that had just popped up that day. *Bother* might be too strong a word; it was more like a nagging thought. *What if he says no?* It never crossed my mind until that very day that there was a possibility that he could say no. *He could say no.* OK, that kind of bothered me, not for the fact that it would say anything about our relationship if he did decline (it would end up just being one of the funny stories we liked to tell), but more for the embarrassment of being turned down in public. To put yourself out there like that in front of everyone, and then have everyone feel sorry for you. But then again, putting myself out there is what I do best. It's the fastest way to create experiences and learn lessons, and I'm an overachiever, baby! During the live taping, I swallowed my fear, accepted that whatever happened was meant to be, went out there, and just tried to have a freaking blast. I was the first to appear, and after my first interview with the host, Eva later said that Sally was ticked because I acted "too funny," and it "wasn't the Stacey show." I felt horrible, and toned myself way down. The way the show was laid out was by segment. After telling our stories, each prospective groom was guided unknowingly to the stage where a black curtain lifted to reveal the cameras, lights, studio audience, and prospective bride standing in the middle of all of the action, throwing out a not-so-witty line, like mine, for example, "Remember that day you said you wished that I could propose to you? [Finger wag] Be very careful what you wish for...." Ugh. It's a horrible line, and I only have myself to blame. Anyway, the next segment was the groom back on the stage with the bride where the brides delivered their sappy proposals. No answer yet, because first they had the groom call a best friend to ask his advice on whether he should or should not marry the bride! Thankfully, that segment never made it to the show, though we felt bad for Dave's friend Troy, as he was excited to be on national TV, giving his advice. Finally, the groom dressed in a tux (no matter the intention), again met the bride on the stage, and walked over to deliver his response. If it was *yes*, the couple took three steps to the bride's right, where a minister immediately started in on the vows as confetti dropped from the ceiling. The couple exchanged rings, and then exited the stage to make room for the next couple. If the answer was *no*, the couple split off and exited the stage on opposite sides to keep the drama to a minimum.

As Dave joined me on the stage to respond to my proposal, I could see in his face that he was going to say yes. I had no doubt…until he began speaking. He mentioned something about how he can't do this, not wanting to do this to our parents, blah, blah, blah. I was trying to process what he was saying when he dropped to his knees and said, "So, I'm going to propose to you"… and then he said something sappy, and asked me to marry him, and I said yes, and we took three steps to the right (his left) and got married in 118 seconds. As we were backstage and unable to see what was happening, we didn't know who got married until couples slowly started trickling back. The girls were giddy, and the guys…if they weren't, they put on a good act. Dave was insanely excited and happy, and I knew I had made the right decision. The last couple was Michelle and her boyfriend. Michelle came off the stage alone, eyes red, before someone swept her away for consolation and counseling. His answer was that he wanted to have a "proper wedding" back home with their families, but I think she knew it was just an excuse, and would never happen. They ended up breaking up after the show, which she later acknowledged as best for her in the long run. She's now pregnant and happily married with an adorable stepson, living on a little farm, baking, cooking, and being a mom. I'm not sure about Tammy, but Deidre is still married to the guy from the show, with two gorgeous kids. I believe everyone else has divorced, but because of the amazing memories, would be shocked if any of them have regrets. As for our fearless leader Sally Ann, she's since created a little show you may have heard of…it's called *Jersey Shore*, bitches!

Going to pick out our dresses!
(l to r) Wendy, Lauren, Eva, Tammy, Deidra, Michelle & me

Surprise Wedding!! Mr. & Mrs. after the show.

Chapter 18

Dave had only had two pets in his entire life…a hamster and a fish…both of which he was deathly afraid of.

The following January, we packed up and moved to good ol' Wichita, Kansas. I knew I wouldn't live there forever, but it was a good home base while we figured out what we wanted to do. Our frustration with San Diego was rooted in the fact that we had been looking at homes only to discover that we wouldn't be able to get away with less than a four-hundred-thousand-dollar mortgage…and that was for a twelve-hundred-square-foot piece-of-crap starter home. My homes in Wichita had been twice as nice and half the price, so that really bugged me! Infuriated me, actually. I felt like someone was trying to rip me off. Also, in order for Dave to get a teaching job, he had to do some postgraduate work to receive his teaching credential, and we weren't exactly rolling in the dough. Unless our lotto numbers came in, twenty percent for a down payment on a house *and* graduate school tuition was the same as impossible.

So we settled nicely back in Wichita. I was working for the crazy lady at the nonprofit, and Dave was working at the Juvenile Detention Facility until he could get his license to teach in Kansas. When our lease ran out six months later, we bought a house in College Hill, a really cool neighborhood with beautiful old homes. Ours wasn't exactly beautiful, but Dave's parents visited shortly thereafter and helped us with some serious home improvements. It was a nice house, but I was never fully comfortable living there. The energy was pretty weird, and it didn't feel like my home. Shortly after we moved in, I found out I was pregnant, and gave the customary, "What the fuck!" response that surely all women say when seeing the + sign on the pregnancy test stick. What? Oh…you didn't say that? Hmm. Maybe it's just me, because I had the exact same response when I saw it with my second pregnancy.

By that time, we had rescued a four-month-old black Lab/mix pup from a shelter (she's laying at my feet, snoring, as I type) that we named "Turises' Midnight Storm." We call her Stormi for short…and Stormi T….and Baby-sissy-puppet-head…and Puppet…and Sis…and Storm…*and* Sissy. She responds to all of the above, poor thing. I first saw Storm when I went with my friend and co-worker, Heather, to the pound to break her own Lab (an accomplished escape artist) out of doggy jail for the two hundredth time. Stormi was crated right next to Heather's dog, so I put my fingers in the cage and started talking to her. She had the most pathetic look on her face, and then she put her nose on my hand and closed her eyes. Aww…my heart broke, and I nearly cried. I asked about her at the front, and they said if she wasn't claimed by the following day, she was free to be adopted. I told Dave about her that night, and he hesitantly agreed to go check her out the following day. Dave had only had two pets in his entire life…a hamster and a fish… both of which he was deathly afraid of. Apparently the hamster always bit him, and the fish had a habit of jumping out of its bowl. I can see why that would be terrifying (not). He also thought my love for animals was totally annoying, and he couldn't understand how I could get so excited when I saw someone with a dog in public. He said I reminded him of a zombie because my eyes would glaze over, and my arms would jut out as I dropped anything I was holding and headed straight to the poor, unsuspecting dog (and owner) to give it some "sugar."

As fate would have it, Stormi captured Dave's heart at first sight, and he brought her home that day. She's been my best friend ever since. She's fiercely protective, and acts like a hall monitor around the house. She likes to step in with a couple of stern-sounding barks when the kids start arguing or fighting with each other, and let me tell you, they listen. I could scream at them at the top of my lungs for five minutes straight, and it wouldn't faze them, but a couple of sharp barks from the pup, and they're suddenly on their best behavior. She's also not afraid to step in front of the kids and "put me in my place" when I'm getting onto them about something. If she doesn't like the tone of my voice or body language I'm directing their way, she stands right between us and gives me her loud doggy lecture. The cats aren't even safe from the hall monitor! God forbid they want to wrestle around with each other. If she's in the room, and they start their WWE kitty moves, she's up in a hot flash giving them a piece of her mind. It's pretty nice to have the extra help, but I think she may have taken the hall monitor status too far the day she chased a poor Girl Scout around our car a dozen or more times, barking like a maniacal animal with her lips peeled back in a snarl. They went around and around the car until finally the poor thing was so tired from running (the Girl Scout, not Stormi), she tripped, rolled onto her back and just lay on the ground trying to catch her breath, not even caring if Stormi was going to eat her. Storm just stood above her, bitching her out, until I finally pulled her by her collar back into the house. I ran back to the little girl, and when she was finally able to speak, she apologized for "freaking out" and then showed me a huge scar where a dog had bitten her a couple of years back! Oh. My. God. Storm bullied the only kid on the block that had already been attacked by a dog! I was mortified, but the kid was totally cool about the whole thing, trying to console *me*! I don't even need to tell you how many boxes of cookies I bought.

Needless to say, mothering Stormi kept me pretty busy, and a baby was not something I was particularly eager for. After watching some of my friends go through motherhood, I didn't think I would ever really be *eager*, and it was probably going to have to just happen on its own, without a lot of effort from me. I knew I eventually wanted to have kids, but I just couldn't make the commitment to actually go forward with it. Kind of like the whole marriage thing…again, I just left it to the universe. Apparently, the universe thought it was time for me to shit or get off the pot, because there I was, sitting in the bathroom with my mom, looking at a stick that said I was pregnant. Shit, indeed.

The pregnancy did absolutely nothing to convince me that getting knocked up was the right road to take. I was miserable. I literally despised being pregnant. I hated every second of it. I was the polar opposite of the "glowing, pregnant lady" and still, to this day, when I see a pregnant woman, I cringe and have to turn away because of how uncomfortable it makes me. How messed up is that? Getting pregnant was the beginning of the end of my life as I knew it. I've never been the same, and if I'm being totally honest, I'll admit that life would have been far easier if I had chosen the childless route. Don't get me wrong—if I had it to do over again, I wouldn't change a thing… but…(deep sigh)…those stories don't belong here.

After quitting my job and deciding to move, we put the house on the market, and it sold the following day. The buyers wanted to close in thirty days, and we couldn't move to Texas until after the baby came, because we needed the insurance and doctor, so we moved into an apartment that offered a month-to-month lease. Apparently, the nicer complexes in town didn't offer that option, so we were stuck in a dirtbag basement apartment with people living above us that had sex constantly. Loud sex. Loud enough that we kept a broom next to our bed so we could knock on the ceiling when it sounded like they were starting to get too carried away. It wasn't long after we moved in that Dave was laid off. There we were. Both unemployed. Baby on the way. Unsavory living accommodations. You name it, it sucked. We didn't know what to do with ourselves. We couldn't sit in the dingy apartment, so we started walking some trails that were nearby. We walked and walked and walked for two months. Thank God, because the way I ate, I would have gained more than the forty-four pounds had I been sitting on my fat, pregnant ass. Those walks turned out to be amazingly therapeutic for us. We became even closer, and with hesitant excitement, started planning for the birth of the baby. We had a lot of changes ahead of us, and I started feeling hopeful for the new phase of our life. Silly me.

It will take another book entirely to explain the chaos that ensued after having Willow and then Nikko. When I say chaos, I'm not talking about "look at this fun, crazy house" kind of chaos. I'm talking "Stacey left the building and was replaced by a robot" chaos. I haven't ever been the same. The pressure and responsibility of kids was more than I ever bargained for, and I lost every little ounce of control I had over my own life, which caused irreparable damages to my psyche and sense of well-being. Having kids meant I was no longer allowed to structure my life the way I wanted to. The kids were in control, a feeling that drove me mad, and added to the resentment I felt at not having control of my body during pregnancy. Life had taken a turn for the worse, and I often wondered who had ever thought it was a good idea for me to be a mother. I love my kids and would do it all again in a second, but those were, hands-down, the hardest times of my life, and I can't believe my husband is still around. It's been almost ten years since that fateful night we got hitched, and we are still crazy about each other. It's no secret that I have a hard time maintaining relationships, but he makes it so easy. It's pretty obvious that he has to put up with a lot of shit when it comes to me, and he always does it with ease and grace. Watching him deal with me makes me want to be a better person, though if I were him, there's no way I'd be able to put up with me. I've told you, it's all I can do sometimes to just put up with myself. I really need to learn how to do those out-of-body experiences, just so I can get a damned break sometimes.

Section Five:
Things That Could Make Me Look Bad

"Be who you are and say what you feel, because those who mind don't matter, and those who matter don't mind."

—Dr. Seuss

Chapter 19

I guess it's not something you stop and think about when you aren't lacking for anything and can scratch your ass.

It would take me forever to explain every quirk that accompanies this kooky noggin, but there are some that stand out as having the potential to be problematic for me or those around me. Some are going to be obvious. For example, I'm forgetful. Duh. Willow calls me "the Forgetter" and is constantly making sure I keep up with everything she brings home from school..."Here, Mom...sign this...I have a test on this tomorrow...I need to bring this library book back on Thursday"...blah, blah, blah. I'm actually thankful, because if I had the extra cash, I would hire an assistant. But I have Willow, who's saving me at least a hundred bucks a day. Unfortunately she's not around me at all times, so on occasion, I'll have a "forgetter" moment like the following doozy.

Our good friends next door, Ken and Becky, aka Babs, were having their annual St. Patrick's Day party. It was getting late, and another of our neighbors, Eunice, was getting ready to walk to her house, which was just across the street. Eunice has to be at least ninety years old. She claims to be in her sixties, but if she's in her sixties, I'm a freaking fetus, and I'm not sure she wasn't drinking shots at the party, so, between the two, I told her I would watch her walk home to make sure she arrived safely. She thanked me and told me it wasn't necessary, but I insisted. In the meantime, Babs' daughter, my good friend Erica, had walked outside. Eunice wasn't even halfway across the street before Erica whispered to me to join her on the side of the house for some adventure or another, and I forgot all about poor old Eunice, shuffling away. I turned and skipped around to Erica. It was probably a good minute later before my stomach fell when I remembered I was supposed to be watching Eunice walk home. I gasped and ran to the front of the house, stopping at the street just as Eunice reached her front door and turned to wave at me. She had no idea I had been MIA for most of her journey. I felt terrible for forgetting about her, but mostly I just couldn't believe it took her that long to cross the street!

The forgetter moment that stands out to me as most publicly embarrassing was the time I forgot the gas nozzle was still in my tank as I drove off. I swear, it was the most wretched sound I have ever heard in my life. The squeal of metal on metal, and then a huge pop as the nozzle was yanked violently out of the pump (apparently a safety feature, but too dramatic for my taste). I ducked, waiting for the explosion. When I finally felt like it was OK to sit up, I looked around at everyone gathered around my car and the newly deformed gas nozzle and pump. You could tell that the onlookers were dumbfounded by my stupidity, and I found myself stricken with the giggles. Fortunately, my insurance covered the damage. Unfortunately, one of the witnesses happened to be the fraternity brother of a guy I was seeing, and the entire WSU campus knew the story before I ever arrived at my first class that morning.

I forget things every day. I can remember something and then forget about it before I even think of writing it down. It's why I find it hard to make lists, I think. I just get little magic poofs of thought, and then they disappear as quickly as they show up—many times before I even process their presence. I recently saw a commercial for an electric car—a 100 percent electric car that didn't need to be filled with $4.32-per-gallon gas. Being a green kind of girl and also cheap, I got really excited. I even imagined myself buying it and driving it around town until I realized, *I can't even keep my phone charged. How in the hell will I remember to keep my car charged?* If your phone isn't charged, big deal…you just can't make a phone call. If your car isn't charged, your ass is stuck in the Target parking lot!

A couple of weeks ago, Dave asked me to get fish food when I got cat food at the pet store. I told him OK. I came home with no fish food. I had forgotten, so I told him that I'd get it in a couple of days when I planned to go back. There was enough to last a couple of weeks, so it wasn't a big deal. A few days later, I was on my way to the pet store when Dave called. I told him where I was going, and he reminded me to get fish food. I was glad that he'd reminded me because, naturally, I'd already forgotten. I let him know that I needed to get off the phone immediately so I could say, "fish food…fish food…fish food" over and over again until I had the fish food in my hand. If I didn't, I was afraid I would forget by the time I got in there. He agreed, we hung up, and I started my mantra, "fish food…fish food…fish food." I'm not sure where in the store I lost focus, but I'm embarrassed to say, I still didn't make it home with the fish food. I forgot again. Dave was annoyed, and I thought it was funny. I was just so amazed by myself that I could have possibly forgotten the fish food after all that effort to remember. It was just *so* bad it was funny. A week later, with considerably less fish food than the previous week, we were running errands when I told Dave that we needed to go to the pet store for cat food. As he dropped me at the front of the store, he reminded me once again to get the fish food and brought up the fact that I had already forgotten twice. I promised him that I could not possibly forget, especially with him in the car, and marched into the pet store, bound and determined to get that damned fish food once and for all. Ten minutes later, I was back in the car telling Dave about the kittens that were up for adoption inside. We had just pulled out of the parking lot when he turned to me and slowly said, "Did you get the fish food?" I swear to you I almost pooped my pants. Can you believe it? I actually forgot the fucking fish food again! Dave was flabbergasted, and I was mortified. He said, "You have a real problem!" My response was, "Uh, yeah, ya think?" I made him turn around so I could redeem myself by actually buying the fish food, which I did, finally. Dave could only shake his head; he couldn't even laugh a little.

Even though forgetting everything sucks for the most part, it does have its advantages. It can create an instant adventure, as one particular episode did (and oddly, this happened when I needed an adventure the most). It was summer and I was in the middle of a funk. As a side note, I've recently figured out that I seem to go into a deep funk at the beginning of summer and don't come out until the fall weather starts. I attribute this to the highly overstimulating Texas sun. I become Edward Cullen, but I don't sparkle…I just get really pissy. The kids and I had just gotten home from swimming lessons, and I was upstairs hanging the towels up to dry when I heard a commotion at my front door. I poked my head over the railing to look through the side windows next to the door, and I saw Dave's feet and two pairs of legs wearing black pants and black shoes. I knew those legs anywhere! Those were the legs of cops! I instantly regressed to my former naughtier self and decided to hide in Nikko's room. As I was crouched in the corner like a criminal, my mind was furiously trying to figure out why they were at my door. Suddenly I had a vision of the bright orange postcard I'd received weeks earlier from a small town near my house stating that I was so overdue on paying a traffic ticket a warrant had been issued for my arrest. Isn't it amazing that even the looming danger of getting arrested with white mineral sunblock smooshed about the face (which made for a lovely mug shot) and kids running around while getting handcuffed wasn't enough to convince my brain that paying that ticket was something worth remembering? Not even worth writing down! How is that possible? The thing is…my brain doesn't ask *my* opinion on what to keep and what to dump from its apparently small storage room. If my brain would have said, "Hey, Stace…do you think I should tell you to write that down on your to-do list, or just forget about it?" I would have said, "Hell yeah, brain! Of course you should tell me to write it down. Why do you even need to ask? Geez!" Unfortunately, thoughts and motivation have to make it by the bouncer (my brain) to get in the door of the club (me). That's what I live with. To top it off, my brain has no idea it's not running on all eight cylinders. It actually thinks it's doing a bang-up job!

As my stomach dropped with the realization that they were there to arrest me, I heard a key in the door. It creaked open slowly, and then Dave yelled, "Staaaacey!" I didn't answer him. I just stayed where I was, frozen. "Staaaacey." At that time, the kids ran out of my bedroom to greet Dave. *Oh no! The kids just gave me away!*

Of course, the kids wouldn't be in the house alone, so surely *Staaaacey* was not far behind. Shit! I'm totally busted! On the third, "Staaaacey," I meagerly replied, "Yeah?"

"The police are here to see you."

"The police? Umm…OK." I felt like I was walking the plank as I descended the stairs to my imminent arrest, scheduled to take place in front of my kids. Nice.

I said hello and invited the officers inside. I asked them if their visit was about the unpaid traffic ticket, and they confirmed it was. I asked them if they were going to arrest me, and they confirmed they were. Shit! It was a male and female officer, and they explained to me that they were in the middle of a "warrant roundup," which entailed knocking on the door of every individual with a warrant out for their arrest, and well…umm…arresting them! I laughed and seriously thought they were kidding. I didn't think there was any way one would waste the time of police officers on something petty like that. They told me they were serious, so I wiped the smile off my face. Apparently warrants are worth big bucks to the city, and the city needed some moola, so voilà. My smile magically reappeared when I noticed that the male officer was wearing short shorts, not unlike Officer Dangle on *Reno 911*. OK, maybe they weren't quite as short as Officer Dangle's, but they were short enough to tickle me! I really got a big kick out of that. They mistook my smile as friendliness and commented that I was the first of their warrants to treat them with kindness and to invite them into the house. They didn't know that ten minutes prior I had been crouching in the corner calling them "stinkin' coppers." It was a good thing they were on my side because I'm not sure anyone else would have had the patience for what ensued.

They told me that I would be booked and released as long as I brought the money to pay my fine. If I didn't have the money, I would be put in the pokey until I did. I figured getting arrested was bad enough, so I agreed to pay the fine. Neither Dave nor I had cash, so the next option was to bring my debit card. Sounds simple enough, but there was a slight problem: my card had expired. Sure, I had the new card I'd received in the mail the month before, but I had absolutely no idea where it was. Apparently my brain didn't think it was worth suggesting that I put it in my purse as soon as it came in the mail. I asked the officers if an expired card would work. They just looked at me. I asked the officers if I could use Dave's card and forge his name. That wasn't an option either. I finally asked them if they could hold on while I searched for the nonexpired card, and they agreed. I tore the house apart. It took me twenty-five minutes to find that thing in one of my piles. When I finally found it, I had to ask the officers if they could wait a bit longer, as I had to call the 1-800 number on the front to activate it. You could tell they were dumbfounded by the complete circus going on in front of them. By then Dave had the kids back upstairs after telling them I was going with the officers to talk about *decorating the police station*. I guess thinking on his feet isn't one of my husband's strengths. Apparently, the kids were OK with that random answer, or SpongeBob was calling their names, because they didn't cause a huge ruckus. With them out of the way, Dave asked the officers if he could take a picture of me with handcuffs on. I'm all for documenting our adventures, so I thought it was a funny idea. I was surprised that the officers agreed so readily, but they did and slipped the cuffs around my wrists so Dave could snap the photo. We all laughed, and I held my arms out in front of me like *OK…that was funny, now take them off*. The two officers looked at each other, and then looked at me, and the female said, "Umm…we can't take those off, ma'am. Handcuffing is required, and normally you would be handcuffed behind your back, but we're trying to be nice." Handcuffed? Behind the back? Really? Sounded a bit dramatic (not "nice") to me, but hey, what do I know? I'm the dumbass getting arrested. As if on cue, the kids came skipping back down the stairs to join in on the fun they just knew they were missing. One officer kindly threw something over the cuffs to hide them from the kids, and they led me out the door toward their car. As soon as I walked outside, I looked over to my right and saw Becky and Erica sitting outside, watching the whole scene go down with their mouths open. Becky looked like she was about to cry and yelled, "Girl, is there anything we can do?" I laughed and told her no and that I'd explain everything when I got back home. I didn't want her to think I was operating a meth lab next door! I had no idea the conversation wouldn't take place until nearly five hours later. Silly me. I thought my adventure was just the getting arrested part!

Their cop car did not disappoint. It was a badass, unmarked, black Dodge Magnum with windows so tinted you could see your future when you tried to look inside. I didn't know how much I would appreciate those windows until we were rolling down Park Avenue, teasing and tempting other motorists to try to get a peek at the criminal in the back of the unmarked, yet completely obvious, cop car. Just another day in the life of a PTA board member! As they opened the door to the backseat and helped me in, I was pleased that they had their hands on top of my head to keep it from bumping—not because I was worried about bumping my head, but because I wanted my arrest to look like the countless arrests I had seen on movies and TV. I didn't want to feel gypped of the experience feeling and looking 100 percent authentic, especially if it was authentic enough to hang out on my record for life! The backseat was a big piece of molded plastic with dips for two butts. Not exactly ergonomic, I would imagine. If they hadn't buckled me in, I would have slid from one side of the car to the other at every turn. Up and down over the butt molds like a seasoned ass-skier gliding effortlessly down the moguls. It wasn't until after they waved good-bye to my family and friends in the front yard and disappeared behind the doors of the badass cop car that they explained we weren't going straight to the station. Apparently only one fugitive roundup at a time isn't economical, so they had three other addresses to hit before heading into the station. I'm not gonna lie: I was excited for the adventure, but I definitely wasn't thrilled about sharing the backseat with another criminal. I wasn't sure the next guy was going to be as fun-loving as I was, and I've seen what people do when they're angry and unable to use their hands or feet—they use their mouths. Biting is worrisome, but even more worrisome for me is the spit! I almost gagged just typing the word. As far as human secretions go, spitting tops my list as the most offensive. I would rather roll around in shit than spit, and I'm not just saying that because it rhymes. I tried to keep my worries at bay by keeping a conversation going with the officers. As we were heading toward the next stand-off, one of them asked me why I didn't pay my fine, especially after getting the orange warrant notice in the mail. The old "I didn't receive it" excuse wasn't going to fly, because as I was searching for my debit card, I came across the bright-orange postcard and they were standing right there to witness it. I'm not sure if it was the irony or just because I was nervous, but that brought on a whole new urge to giggle when I held it up, prompting the usual puzzled look I receive from most people on most days. As being honest is as much a part of me as being forgetful, I just explained to them that I had put it in one of my piles and forgotten about it. They seemed to believe me and said it was refreshing for me to take responsibility for my actions and the consequences. It wasn't long after that that they named me the "Zen Criminal." I begged them to put that on my record as one of my aliases, but they just laughed. Dang it! I was serious! Suddenly we were crawling through another neighborhood, trying to find the address of the next unsuspecting warrant-ignorer. As they pulled up to the house, my heart was going crazy, but my brain was lit up like a million missiles were exploding in every corner, dumping tons of adrenaline, serotonin, and dopamine. At that moment my usual sludge brain was working like a fine piece of newly greased machinery, in perfect harmony with every part of itself. I almost felt high. Not like a weed high. More like "I can fly" high…though not like the PCP kind of "I can fly" (that after-school special scared the crap out of me)…like….umm…well, the drug analogy isn't really working for me, so let's just say, at that moment, I was 100 percent chemically, mentally, and emotionally in balance. It was the most amazing feeling. I felt so free and weightless and, God forbid, I felt…could it be…I believe it is…*happy*! I felt the emotion of happiness, a very rare emotion for me, due only to the chemistry in my brain. I often wonder if that's what normal people feel like all the time. Not necessarily happy, but just without constant angst, depression, and anxiety. If so, I really hope they're able to appreciate it. I kind of doubt it, though. Just like I don't appreciate it that I have my hearing, sight, or the ability to scratch my butt when it itches, thanks to my limbs. I guess it's not something you stop and think about when you aren't lacking for anything and can scratch your ass.

As the male officer was getting out, he started pulling the keys from the ignition, and then looked at me in the backseat. It was one hundred–plus degrees out, and the back windows didn't open. My booty was already sticking to the seat, and I was not willing to leave this earth by accidental heat suffocation during a warrant roundup in the back of a cop car, no matter how badass it was. He asked me if I was going to run. I laughed, raising my cuffed wrists to point to my head and said, "not likely," referring to my greasy ponytail and the white mineral sunblock still coating my face from the earlier swimming lessons. He explained that it was completely against the rules to leave the keys in the car and it would cost him his job if I took advantage of the situation. I assured him that I was entirely too lazy to run and was looking forward to the next couple of arrests, as I considered myself their sidekick at that point. He laughed and closed the door with the blessed air-conditioner running. I got as comfortable as I could so I could fully enjoy the view from the other side.

My mouth dropped as both cops immediately went into full SWAT mode, running to either side of the house with their hands on their guns. The female inched toward the front, ducking under windows, while the male stayed close to the house, following it toward the back. What the hell were they doing? Did they act this dramatically at my house? It looked like some serious shit was going down. I'm talking hostage situation or bomb threat—not a warrant for unpaid fines! My armpits started itching from the adrenaline, and I sunk lower in my seat, yet not so low that I couldn't see the action, not knowing if a crazy, gun-toting redneck was going to start shooting his sawed-off shotgun through his living room window. Why would they take me to pick up such a dangerous fugitive? Suddenly, I recalled Becky's face as I was led from the house, almost in tears, and realized, yes, they did do this crazy shit at my house too! I watched as the female cop knocked on the front door, stepping to the side quickly, and I thought, *Man, I don't blame them*. They probably get bored out of their minds policing their sleepy town, and that's a way to keep the excitement in their jobs. If I were them, I would do the same thing. Even if I was just on traffic duty, I would wave the cars by with my gun, and every now and then drop and roll in the middle of the street, coming up on my knee with my gun pointing at one of the intersections to let them know it was their turn to move. After a couple of minutes of nobody answering the door (duh…my plan too, but it failed when the kids broke my cover), they gave up and came back to the car. They looked slightly dejected, and I kind of felt sorry for them. I even felt a twinge of disappointment after finally psyching myself up to be caged in the backseat with my town's version of Jeffrey Dahmer. I told them not to worry, that we'd get the next one. They laughed and thanked me for not running or stealing the car. As we were driving to the next *Reno 911* call, I worked up the courage to ask them if they were just messing around when they inched up on the last house like it was an underground lab full of naked coke-making ladies, or if it was protocol. That garnered the biggest laugh of the day, and they assured me that it was indeed protocol, and once again they explained that most of the people they picked up didn't have quite sunny personalities. So much for my boredom theory. I took that as a sick compliment and started psyching myself up for the next house.

I think we all got kind of excited when we pulled up to the next house and saw three cars in the driveway. You can't have three cars in the driveway with nobody home! The cops left the keys in the car and started their Rambo Mamba up to the house. I have to admit, they looked pretty cool, and I can't say that I didn't ponder the possibility of becoming an officer of the law at that moment. Suddenly, my arms and legs were covered with goose bumps, not just from the excitement, but from the incredible amount of respect and gratitude that washed over me as I realized how much police officers risk every day to keep us safe. It almost made me cry as I thought about the call that the female officer had received on her cell phone while we were en route: it was her twelve-year-old daughter checking in and asking what they were having for dinner. They ended the conversation with an "I love you." That's all. Seemingly a simple and basic conversation, but in retrospect, it had so much more meaning because statistics show that a police officer has a good chance of one day not making it home to cook dinner that night, or any night thereafter. I can't stand the thought of it. Thinking about that little girl still makes me want to cry. Even with all this wackiness in my head, at least I'm not worrying that my kids may one day not have me yelling at them. My heart overflows with love and gratitude for those that serve and protect us: the police officers, hot firefighters, military personnel, doctors (a slightly more complicated relationship), astronauts, and so on. I feel so much love for these humans, I could burst…either that or I'm attracted to a dude in a uniform. In any case, to all of my beautiful heroes, I give you my heart. It's not a lot, but it's the best damned thing I own.

Unfortunately or fortunately (depending on your take), the house didn't yield any previously mentioned gun-toting rednecks or a kindly grandmother in the midst of baking a pie. (I met her at the station while we were both waiting to get fingerprinted. She gave the "I just forgot" reason as well, but at least she had age on her side.) Nobody answered, so they trudged back to the car, beat down by defeat and Texas humidity. Before they were even in the car, I exclaimed, "That's bullshit! There are three cars in the driveway! You know they're home and just not answering the door!" (For a second I actually forgot I was guilty of the same and was not a fully licensed officer of the law.) They both chuckled. "What if I wouldn't have answered the door?" They told me I didn't have to. The timing had been perfect: they rolled up, and Dave pulled up a few seconds after. Of course, he didn't notice the intimidating black car with 100 percent tint idling just ten feet away from him. Thank God a molester never drove by his house when he was a little kid playing in the front yard—he wouldn't have stood a chance! Apparently, my not-so-aware husband was heading up the front walk when they jumped out and did a SWAT side-swipe maneuver, each one coming up on either side of him, asking him if Stacey Turis lived there and scaring the crap out of him while he tried to gain composure and hold on to the takeout he was surprising me with. You know the story from there…

Unfortunately for the 5-0 and their trusty sidekick, the third house was also a dud. They finally got on the radio and informed dispatch that they were bringing "Stacey Turis" in for a warrant. I had to stifle a giggle hearing my name like that. About fifteen minutes later, we pulled up to the station. I suddenly got nervous and asked if people were going to see me. The female officer laughed and said, "Yeah, and they'll all stare at you, too." That was funny until she led me through the back door, which just so happened to open right into the meeting room. There was a shift change happening, so all of the (hot) officers were seated at a huge conference table as their supervisor went over details from that day. Sure enough, every one of them turned to look at me. I was less upset by the fact that I was coming in arrested and more by the fact that I looked like shit. I smiled, raised my cuffs, and waved hi as I was led to the booking room, silently cursing mineral sunblocks and their inability to rub in all the way.

The whole booking process takes forever. It was mostly a blur and pretty uneventful as they filled out paperwork and had me fingerprinted. That's where I met the pie-baking grandmother, so we had a little chat, sharing war wounds, and then I was off to get my mug shot taken. I can't lie: I was actually excited for the mug shot, and I silently obsessed over whether I would be able to receive a copy of it to officially document my adventure. I'll give you a little hint: it's now displayed proudly on my Facebook page. The chief was taking the mug shots, and he was a character. One of the officers said, "Chief? How did you get stuck with mug shot duty?"

He grumbled back, "Ohhh, I can't let you kids have all the fun." He asked me why I hadn't paid the ticket, so I told him, and then I proceeded to explain that I was so glad I had gotten arrested, as it was the most fun I had had in a long time. I gave him a blow-by-blow of the *Reno 911* adventures, which he got a kick out of…especially when I was reenacting his officers' SWAT moves. I finally shut up long enough for him to direct me behind a chain link fence, where I was told to stand facing the chief and a camera. He took the front-facing shot and immediately began laughing as he looked at the photo on his monitor. He actually had me walk out of the fence room, around a huge counter, and behind a desk to stand by him on the "good-guy" side of the camera, just so I could see how funny my mug shot was. I don't remember now why it was so funny, maybe because I was really trying to look like a hardened criminal, but I do know it was bad enough that he had to retake it. I was more successful on the side-view shot, and bid the chief adieu as I was directed to the window where I could pay the fine and finally get released. My poor brother had been waiting for me for three hours, not knowing when I would emerge with my new record. I handed my newly activated debit card to the lady behind the window to cover the $257 fine and almost pooped right in my pants when she came back with the word "declined." I explained to her that I just activated the card before I left, and she nodded and said, "Oh, well that's it then. They usually decline the first use. We'll run it again." Declined. Oh my God! If I wasn't able to pay, I'd have to book a night in the uberluxurious, small-town jail! Thankfully my brother stepped up and paid my fine, so I could sleep in my own bed that night. When we finally pulled up to my house, Dave was next door at Ken and Becky's with the kids, Erica, and Erica's son. They were all sitting in the front yard, so I got out of my brother's car and headed their direction, knowing I wouldn't be seeing my previously mentioned bed for a while. The whole ordeal made for some good storytelling and laughs that evening, and thanks to the adventure and stimulation, I was high on life, and able to stay out of the dead place for a couple of months. Interesting tidbit: I've since found out that I can also force myself out of the dead place by riding roller coasters, which drives Carrie (my only other rollercoaster companion besides my husband) mad, as I will want to ride them twenty-two times in a row and still want more. It causes embarrassing public fights between us, because it makes her neck so sore, she thinks her head will pop off, but I feel so incredibly good after getting off the ride, it's worth the public humility to feel it over and over again. It's like my serotonin and dopamine are lacking so much, when I get a little drop, I'm like an instant meth-head. If I don't watch myself, I'll be cutting in front of grannies and little kids to get my fix.

It's all fun and games until he leaves the cuffs on.

Warrant Roundup

My mug shot. Yes, I'm proud.

Chapter 20

I flapped around like a crazed maniac, causing hot wax to fly all over my arms and back. I threw myself under the water, not knowing exactly how much on fire my hair really was.

I suppose it would be fair to say that, at times, I can be somewhat distracted and not entirely engaged in my surroundings. Apparently this can cause issues in the world still happening around me. A good example would be the day I was driving down the interstate. I was completely within my mind, and for some reason, designing a yoga studio. I could see every detail clearly as I created this virtual studio. I was so engrossed with designing this nonexistent studio, I probably shouldn't have been driving. Apparently a cop agreed with me, and I was yanked back to reality by the sound of a siren behind me. I could tell the guy was pissed when he walked up. He said that he'd been following me for three miles with his siren and lights going, and wanted to know why I didn't pull over. I explained to him that I honestly had not seen or heard him. I was surprised when he nodded and said, "I could tell...you weren't paying attention at all." He informed me that I had been going fifteen miles over the speed limit, and wanted to know why I was driving so spaced out. Without thinking, I told him that I had been designing a yoga studio in my head. He gave me the familiar puzzled look, told me that was the first time he had ever heard that excuse, and let me off the hook.

Sometimes I'm not so lucky. It was January 1, and we had just put the kids to bed after a particularly long year. Dave poured us each a glass of Champagne, lit the candles around the tub, and ran a steaming hot bubble bath. Taking a bath together is a rarity, because I want the water to be so hot it scalds me, and Dave shies away from intentionally burning himself, so he sticks with regular hot water. In any case, this was a celebration, and he loves to make me happy, so he cupped his package, and lowered himself into the boiling cauldron. I stepped in after him, my back on the opposite side of the tub. Our goal was to come up with our new family saying for the year, which we would then get printed on our checks. This particular night, I was exhausted and didn't think twice about laying my head against the back of the tub to try to engage my thinking cap. I had no idea what I had gotten myself into until Dave sat up, pointing at my head with a horrified look, and yelled "Oh my God! Your fucking hair is on fire!" I flapped around like a crazed maniac, causing hot wax to fly all over my arms and back. I threw myself under the water, not knowing exactly how much on fire my hair really was. When my head and hair were fully submerged, I felt confident that the fire was out. I sat up gasping for air, and Dave hurriedly ran his fingers around my head, trying to find the bald spot that surely wrapped around the back of my skull. Lucky for me, there was no bald spot—just a couple of singed hairs that I later cut out. As soon as we knew my biggest injuries were going to be the wax burns, we lost our minds with laughter. Most of the time, I just have to find the humor in my being a dumbass. We must have belly-laughed for a good forty-five minutes from that unexpected chaos, and scored our new family saying at the same time. For that year, our checks read, "Here's to not catching our hair on fire."

The whole linear time thing is a hard one for me. I actually have no concept of time, past or future. I can hang on to about two weeks of my life, but any event after that gets lumped into *the past*. I also find it impossible to think about, let alone focus on, the future, which explains why I'm always surprised when a holiday or birthday, or any day for that matter, pops up. I'm only comfortably able to look ahead about twenty-four to forty-eight hours in advance without getting overwhelmed and anxious, with less than twenty-four hours being my comfort zone. Anything farther out than that isn't even on my horizon, and to be honest, I work best hour by hour. All of that could make a person seem unorganized, which I am, but mostly it's my ability to live in the present that makes me seem unprepared or a procrastinator, which I am both actually, but what I'm trying to say is that this whole *time* thing doesn't help any of that. I try to feel better about it by telling myself that I must intuitively know that there is no such thing as linear time, so there's no point in trying to follow it! Sometimes it sucks, though, as it leaves little ability for me to get excited about things that are coming up and not within my focus timeframe of twenty-four hours or less. It's actually impossible, but I don't want to bitch about it too much, because as I've said before, some people try their whole lives to learn to live in the present, and I just happened to be born that way, so to me, it's a gift. To those around me, not so much, but that's pretty much the story of my life. Unfortunately, it's taken me until just a couple of years ago to learn how to not give a shit about what other people think. If only I would have learned that trick earlier! I say that, but I also know that it took different lessons for me to come to that conclusion, and I think you have to come by it honestly to really implement it in your life.

Another quirk I have to deal with is my sensitivities. Physical and emotional sensitivities are things I cope with on a daily basis. Physically, I'm sensitive to taste, touch, sound, smell, sight, and the emotions and intentions of others. My body is also really sensitive to medicine and things that touch my skin, most notably poisonous foliage and the chemicals in products. I don't even have to touch Poison Ivy or Poison Oak; I can just walk by and end up with a rash full of weeping bumps. To make matters worse, I'm allergic to any medicine you would put on a rash. It's really a pain in the ass, but for the reasons above, I've learned the value of alternative medicine and cures. The conventional ways cause me more grief and pain than the actual ailment itself!

I'm also sensitive in the conventional sense. The part of me that isn't entirely numb can be easily moved to tears. As Willow's homeroom mom, I was in charge of getting the parties together for the class. At our Valentine's Day party, we were going to make Valentines for the troops, and I knew I would cry when I was explaining it to the kids, so I had to ask one of the other moms to step in. As an Air Force brat, I'm incredibly patriotic and have such respect and love for those that serve our country that just the sight of a uniform can make me cry. I went to the Kennedy Space Center in Cocoa Beach and sobbed the entire time I was there. I couldn't even enjoy it, because the emotions were so intense. It was the same when I visited the Vietnam Veterans Memorial Wall. Just last week, I was at the kids' school, getting ready to read a book about grandparents to some third graders, and was mortified when I was brought to tears from the first page of the book the librarian gave me to read. With red, watery eyes, I had to look like a complete idiot, asking the librarian if I could read a *different* grandparent book, as the one I was holding made me cry. Feeling so much is so exhausting, sometimes unbearable, and I almost think that's why I have learned to turn my emotions off. Unfortunately, that *all or nothing* comes into play, and I'm not able to come to understand the whole "happy medium" concept, so I'm either on or off… open or closed…emotional or simply existing. There's no schedule for it either. I don't get an Excel spreadsheet sent to me the week before letting me know which part of me will be around on which days. I wish I did! That would help my family immensely. I, on the other hand, would never remember to look at the spreadsheet anyway!

Chapter 21

It's only my wisdom and maturity that keep me from regressing to that former-self and styling a "Stone Cold Stunner" on their asses.

As much kindness is in my heart, there's also a small area that constantly simmers with frustration. At times it can reach a boiling level that will easily manifest into angry outbursts, especially if my tolerance level and coping skills are not at their best. I read somewhere that 85 percent of those with AD(H)D suffer from bouts of rage   not anger, *rage*. Imagine the number of people in prison right now that simply need AD(H)D supplements or meds! Though my family has been witness to its share of these outbursts, they are mostly directed toward strangers, especially stupid, judgmental, inconsiderate strangers. Honesty and fairness are incredibly, obsessively important to me, and if I witness something to the contrary, hold on to your britches. My mouth opens, and words spike out like an automatic weapon. At the same time, my hands begin shaking, and my heart gallops heavily in my throat. I have no control over my words, and I am driven by an invisible piece of machinery. I call it my "stranger anger."

The first thing that happens is the "calling out." If I see anyone in a public place guilty of the above offenses, I immediately call them out on it, right to their face, in front of everyone. I'm not sure why I have that reaction. In my mind (consider the source), if I bring it to their attention, they'll be less likely to do it to someone else in the future. For example, I was at a gas station and had been waiting patiently behind a car as the owner finished pumping his gas. He started to pull out and a lady swooped in and took the spot as I gave the other car room to pull out. Holy shit! I was so insta-pissed, I could have seriously jumped out of the car and kicked her fifty-year-old ass. Fortunately for her, I've read Thich Nhat Hanh's book, *Anger*, so instead, I rolled up to her, opened my window, and waited for her to get out. She saw me and acted like she was trying to find something in her purse. I was still waiting when she finally got up the nerve to get out of the car.

Me: Why would you do something like that?

Her: Like what?

Me: Like take that spot when you saw me waiting for it.

Her: Fuck you, bitch.

Me: Umm…Huh?

Her: I said fuck you. You're a bitch.

Brain: *Holy shit! Kick her ass!* No! She's a good 285 pounds…she'd kill me! *No way, you're a lot faster!* But she has gross, bleached hair, cuts in line, says, "Fuck you, bitch" to complete strangers and keeps her cigarettes on her dash. *Oh shit. Yeah…you're probably right…she'd totally kick your ass.*

Me: Well, I see you're classy, as well!

The reason that incident stands out in my head is because afterward, I was so incredibly proud of myself for maintaining control and not losing my cool. I completed my mission, which was to call her out, but I maintained some sort of integrity at the same time. That's huge, because normally after I really lose my cool, I feel immensely guilty for two or three days after the incident, whether the person deserved it or not (who are we kidding; they always deserve it). I just hate the fact that I sort of lose control, so after the gas station incident, I finally felt there was some hope in getting a leash on the impulsivity that always seemed to get me in trouble.

It's those everyday, inconsiderate acts that really piss me off. Someone cuts in line, a salesperson acts bitchy, or even...umm...police officers blocking the streets. Talk about a bad day. I lost my temper with no provocation whatsoever. There are at least fifteen different entrances to my neighborhood, and one day, there were cones blocking all but one. Unfortunately, they didn't leave a sign explaining which one was open, so you just had to drive around aimlessly, hitting dead end after dead end. Not cool for a person that detests not being in control. I was driving around, trying to find a way out, getting more pissed by the second. By the time I found the only open exit, which happened to be manned by four or five police officers, I was so furious that I rolled down my window and basically screamed at them the entire time I was driving by. I have no idea what I said or if it was even intelligible. Shortly thereafter I broke into tears from the trauma of someone throwing a monkey wrench in my day.

I have a gazillion "stranger anger" stories, but you get the idea. You're probably wondering how I could possibly think that screaming my brains out at a bunch of cops for no reason was a good idea. I've since learned to put a leash on my impulsive anger issues because there was a time when *smart me* wasn't around to discourage me from trying to kick someone's ass, and I dealt with those feelings by fighting. Lots of fighting. They were mostly bar fights, though I was in four or five fights in high school. I'll never forget the first fight I was in; I was walking down the hall at school, just minding my own business, when I started hearing the murmurings of a fight. If a fight was scheduled, it didn't take long for the message to make it through the grapevine. As I walked by, every third person I passed would whisper, "Fight. 3:20. Buffalo Park." For some reason, most fights were scheduled to take place at Buffalo Park, and 3:20 p.m. was the quickest we could get there after school let out. I made a mental note to attend the fight and probably somewhat looked forward to it. After all, it was something different to spice up the afternoon, and I was always looking for spice. It took me about an hour to figure out that *I* was actually one of the two participants in the fight. Apparently Jill, one of my best friends from seventh grade, wanted to kick my butt. It was so random, and I had no idea why she would want to do something like that (as I hadn't even talked to her in a couple of years), but I did know one thing: I couldn't back down. I was scared out of my mind, but it never crossed my mind to back down. I still, to this day, wonder why I didn't just say, "Umm…I don't really want to fight, actually." Maybe it was pride; maybe it was stupidity. Whichever it was, my friend Danele and I showed up to the fight at 3:25, and I'm pretty sure the entire school was in attendance. Jill was standing in the middle of the group just waiting to kick my ass as I was pulling up to the park, just waiting to get my ass kicked. I stepped out of Danele's truck, and the crowd parted like the Red Sea. Jill didn't waste time with explanations but instead went into full butt-whooping mode. I don't remember hitting the ground, but suddenly there I was, lying on the grass. There was a lot of commotion on top of me, but I wasn't receiving any of the blows that were obviously being administered. I finally got my wits about me and disentangled myself from two other sets of arms and legs. As I got to my feet, I was shocked to see that the fight had gone another direction, and I wasn't involved! Apparently one of my friends, Susie, saw that I was "smelling what the Rock was cooking" and decided to help me out. Suddenly, Susie was pinning Jill down, yelling, "Kick her! Kick her! Kick her!" I was so new to the "fight" game, I didn't even know she was talking to me until someone nudged me forward saying, "Go on! Kick her!" I moved forward, and started swinging my foot back and forth at her legs. I couldn't stand the thought of kicking her somewhere tender (for example, the ribs, where the mob was directing me), and I felt like such a beast kicking her while Susie held her down. It was really half-hearted on my part, because I felt no animosity toward this girl I had been such good friends with. Sure, she had become kind of scary and hung out with some questionable characters, but that never took away from the fond memories I had of her and I hanging out and causing trouble (a weekly routine of ours was to go to church with her parents, and instead of going to the youth class, we would hide out under the baptism tub, laughing at the people we could hear on the other side. The prize? Breakfast at Grandy's for being the good, little churchgoers her parents thought we were). I walked away from that fight unscathed except for my foot, which I had injured by kicking Jill in the legs. I also walked away with a newfound confidence, because I had taken some blows and realized that in the midst of a fight, with the adrenaline pumping, you don't even feel those blows! There was no pain or fear at all! It made me feel incredibly powerful, like there was nothing to ever be afraid of, and, in a sense, it created a monster. It was at that moment that I learned that I didn't have to ever feel bullied again, because I was capable of fighting back without having to be afraid of pain…figuratively and literally. I used that tool over and over again after that day—in high school, college, and beyond. Most of the fights were a result of someone messing with me or one of my friends. It became a habit, an instant reaction, whereas once I would have hit them with just my sharp wit instead of a right hook (hair-pulling is for pussies). I had a signature move where I would put a foot behind the "perpetrator," and then grab their neck, pushing them backward so they tripped, and I was instantly on top, choking them. Who does that? Who comes up with their own move? As Christa was my partner in crime, and we went out most nights of the week, which statistically increased our chances of a brawl, her job was to grab my shoes as I kicked them off to fight. Yes, not only did I have a signature move, I had an assistant shoe grabber, which took any pressure off of me to try to fight and keep track of my beloved Birkenstocks at the same time. Fighting was my game until I got the job hosting *Flash TV*. Even I knew a public figure (I use that term loosely) couldn't go around getting in bar fights! That was back in the day when "bad publicity" was "bad publicity"—a sex tape would mean the end of my career, as opposed to being the catalyst in launching it. Thanks to ex–news anchor Mogie Langston, anyone in Wichita could have told you that! Hosting that show meant a great deal to me, as it was enough of a motivator to make bar fights (and getting too hammered to walk) a thing of the past instead of the usual weekend entertainment.

I would love to say that I can't fathom being the aggressive person I was, but when that *stranger anger* kicks in, it's only my wisdom and maturity (again, I use both terms loosely) that keep me from regressing to my former self and styling a "Stone Cold Stunner" on their asses. Lately, I've even been keeping my mouth shut. For example, the other day in Target I was waiting in line forever, and was next in line to check out, when they opened up a new register and the new cashier summoned for the lady behind me, instead of me. My blood instantly boiled, and my mouth fell open, not knowing who to hurl my word-daggers at first, when I suddenly got a grip on my impulsivity and closed my mouth. It took me a good two minutes of talking to myself in my head before I felt like my anger was in control, and I could let go of it. I have to say, I'm so glad I did, because again, instead of feeling the usual regret after ripping someone, which would plague me at least all day, I felt pride that I was able to control myself, and let the whole matter go instantly. Baby steps, man! Baby steps!

Chapter 22

Breakfast? Are you shitting me? Can't you see I'm having a near-death experience here?

As you can begin to imagine, there's a lot of riffraff that goes on in this head of mine, and that riffraff interferes with my ability to be a normal person. It also means that I have to be able to cope with living in a constant state of sensory stimulation and chaos. As I've told you, some days I have more coping skills than others, and on those other days, I occasionally use other means to cope, because not coping is simply not an alternative when I'm trying to take care of my family. "Cutting" would be the first coping mechanism I can remember using. Alcohol took the place of cutting when I was fifteen, and weed took the place of alcohol when I was twenty-one…well, I actually drank alcohol *and* smoked weed until I was about thirty. Somewhere in all that, I chewed tobacco for about nine years. Skoal, straight, long cut. Nine years. I can't even believe it myself! I would chew that stuff at bars, not giving a crap who saw me. I carried a spit cup around wherever I went! And the worst part? The guys at the bars totally dug it! You may be wondering how that possibly happened. It all started innocently enough. In college, my friends and I would sometimes indulge in clove cigarettes. One day, I ended up with pneumonia, and for a while couldn't even look at a clove. Not too long after, my friend Melissa and I were on a road trip to Orlando to meet the lead singer of Cameo (*Word Up!*), Larry Blackmon, at his apartment. If you've ever had a bad habit, you know how appealing it is to bust it out while on a long drive…especially if you're the driver. Melissa was in the passenger seat, glamorously puffing away on a clove, and I was salivating at the smell. Smoking cloves is what you do on road trips, dammit! I really wanted one, but I was still traumatized from the pneumonia and didn't want to piss off my tender lungs. My fabulous brain came up with the idea that I should try some chewing tobacco. God knows from living in Kansas I had seen enough people do it. I stopped at the next gas station and bought my first of a gazillion cans.

I tapped the can, like I'd seen done millions of times. After finally figuring out how to open the damned thing, I pinched a big wad of tobacco together, and stuffed in my lower lip. Holy mother of bad habits! It was awesome— like a party in my mouth! It tasted exactly as it smelled, and there was a massive burning sensation where the tobacco rested between my lip and gum. You'd think a massive burning sensation would sound unappealing, but I couldn't get enough of it. I loved feeling the burn, and enjoyed it immensely for too long afterward!

Let me get back to the Cameo story, because that's not just something you throw out there as a side note and then move on…

Melissa and her family lived in the UK when she was growing up. She and her sister happened to meet Larry after one his concerts and they struck up a friendship, but she was a kid. Fast forward to years later; Cameo is scheduled to appear in Wichita. Melissa and her sister go to the concert, and afterward an autograph signing, where Larry remembers them. Melissa gave him her phone number, and they began to occasionally chat on the phone. He lived in Orlando, only three and a half hours away from my mom.

Not long after, Melissa, my brother, and I flew to Florida to hang out with my Mom and Bob. That's the flight I smuggled weed on, in my underwear… have I told you that story? Oh well, it's really not important…plus, my mom's going to be pissed when she reads that.

Melissa was still in touch with Larry, and there were solid plans for us to make a road trip up to see him. We rented a car and told my mom we would be back the following day. She was excited for our adventure with whom she called "Rasta-Man." We found his apartment in Orlando and were greeted with huge hugs. I was instantly comfortable around him and felt nothing but peaceful vibes radiating from his large frame. I later found out those vibes were actually wafts of recently smoked weed. Whatever. He invited us in, and we immediately smoked out. Within the half-hour, he was laughing so hard he had tears pouring down his face. He claimed to have not laughed that hard since he was ten years old, which Melissa and I regarded as a high compliment. I remember him playing his guitar for a bit, and then we were, of course, famished. We somehow ended up at Applebee's, and were immediately greeted with scowls when a couple of girls recognized Larry. They made it pretty apparent that they didn't like the fact that he was hanging out with white girls, which of course caused a whole new slew of giggles to erupt from all three of us. I can honestly say that we never stopped laughing the entire time we were in Applebee's. Not only did we find the "white girl" thing funny, but the waitress sat us next to the TV, which was showing an *America's Funniest Home Videos* marathon. If you've ever seen it, you know that you'll laugh your ass off at that show stone-cold sober. Well, that night we made a downright ruckus, we were laughing so hard. I'm not even sure how long we sat there in hysterics, but it was a long time before we were even able to get ourselves together to look at the menu and order. I can't imagine what our poor waitress thought.

We were all exhausted from the Applebee's experience and decided to head back to Larry's apartment. Again, we smoked out, and he played his guitar. I remember he had a lot of supplements on his counter and was shocked to learn he took "shark cartilage." I thought it was weird, which translated to cool, so I made him explain what each one did. I think that was my real introduction to herbs and supplements. My mom has always made us take vitamins, but I found it more of a pain in the ass than anything. When he explained to me what actually occurs in the body as a result of all of those gag-inducing horse pills, I was fascinated, and I'm now the weirdo with all of the supplements on the counter.

The next morning we had to rush home in order to see Bob before he left on a trip. We bid sweet adieu to our Rasta-man, and hit the road at top speed. I, of course, had a humongous wad of Skoal in my mouth when we first heard the siren behind us. Cops! D'oh! I was signaled over and was too scared to spit the Skoal out, for fear the officer would think I was up to something worse if he saw my actions from behind. He ended up being a pretty cool dude, and thought my tobacco-chewing was "adorable" (I'm batting my eyes as I write). Come to think of it, he still gave me a speeding ticket, so it must have not been that adorable! We made the most of the experience and took pictures with the poor guy, promising to send them to his precinct. We thought that would be the last we saw of him, but not forty-five minutes down the road, he was once again parked behind us on the side of the road with his lights flashing, only this time we weren't pulled over…we actually ran out of gas. It must have been his lucky day, as he was once again blessed with our charm as he drove us to the nearest gas station…me still with a dip in my mouth.

Road Trip! This cop was so nice, we hung out twice!

Hanging out with Larry Blackmon from the group, Cameo.

Thankfully, I came to the conclusion that it was a disgusting habit, especially for a person who loathes spit, and I quit cold turkey. I have since learned that I can get the same hand-to-mouth fix by eating pomegranates. Who knew? Anyway, it wasn't until I became pregnant with Willow that I had the motivation to stop coping by less-than-positive means. I've done fairly well since. I rarely drink and I can proudly say I no longer cut myself on the face or chew tobacco, but I'd be a lying dog if I said I didn't occasionally smoke some weed with friends. What can I say? There's nothing on the face of the earth that relaxes and calms me more than weed…as some of you may enjoy a nice glass of Cabernet can relate. The only difference is that wine is legal and marijuana should be. Marijuana is as much of a gateway to harder drugs as a sip of wine can lead to drinking mouthwash to get your alcohol fix. It can happen, but it all depends on the person. What I find frightening is the legality of *prescription drugs*. Now that's some scary shit! Nobody has ever died of a marijuana overdose, but people keel over every day from mixing common drugs prescribed by their family doctor! That's just the legal stuff…imagine all of the crap they're making on the streets in dirty bathtubs! I've seen enough after-school specials to know that if I try heroin, I'll instantly die, and if I try meth, I'll be hooked for life and lose my teeth. I did try cocaine once, and that was a letdown. Since it's a stimulant, and I have AD(H)D, it just made me feel more focused, which is why a lot of AD(H)D sufferers turn to cocaine. I figure I can just take my legal medicine and get the same effect without rotting out my nasal cavity. I also did ecstasy once. That was cool for the first twelve hours until I wanted to go to sleep. Then, when I tried to close my eyes, the room would appear so bright I would have to open my eyes to keep from getting blinded by the light behind my closed lids. That sucked enough for me to forget the fun part. I also tried acid. I sucked on that little Mickey Mouse stamp for a good two hours (it never disintegrated, and I finally just swallowed it), and nothing ever happened. I took that as a sign that I probably shouldn't be doing it, and never tried again. Today, I'm sure my brain thanks me for it.

Though none of my experiences with chemical drugs have turned out to be positive, I have to say, the worst drug experience of my whole life was not from doing drugs, but getting drugged. If you've ever seen *The Hangover*, you know exactly what I'm talking about. The only thing missing from my version was the tiger, and I can't even be entirely sure there *wasn't* a tiger involved.

It was Carrie's birthday, and since I'd been living in San Diego the previous couple of years, we were bound and determined to make it memorable, which now seems kind of ironic, since we don't remember most of it. We dressed up in our slickest "going out in Wichita" outfits, and headed downtown to our favorite haunt, Heroes. Heroes was all-around awesome on Saturday nights thanks to their karaoke. We had to get there early to secure a booth, so we plopped our butts in a prime location at about 6:45 p.m. Our plan was to pace ourselves, as we wanted to stop drinking in time to be able to drive home sober. We started off with a nice little Blow Job shot, explaining to the bartender that we had a birthday girl (expecting to get our Blow Jobs for free, as crass as that sounds...which we did). The DJ helped our cause by announcing Carrie's birthday. Wichita had a population of four hundred thousand-plus, but the dynamics were that of a small town, so we always knew at least a third of the people in any given bar, all of whom were eager to help celebrate anything by buying rounds of shots. After the DJ's announcement, even strangers stepped in, bringing alcohol and birthday wishes to the table. We didn't drink a majority of the birthday shots, as a couple of weeks prior we had gotten in a bit of trouble from Carrie's husband, Mike, after arriving at her home at 2:30 a.m. to deliver her crumpled on the floor of the backseat after a night of partying. Since Carrie was unconscious at the time, I received most of the wrath from Mike, and I wasn't looking forward to a repeat performance that evening. I don't want to mislead you by acting like we weren't getting a little tipsy. We were definitely feeling good, and as the night drew on, the bar started filling up. It wasn't before long that there was barely enough room to walk to the bathroom. In all of her Carrie glory, my friend decided that would be a good time to start swing dancing with complete strangers and no regards to toes or angry, chubby girls with a distaste for fun-loving skinny ones. I was apologizing left and right as Carrie sang Happy Birthday to herself, whirling like the Tasmanian devil, causing just as much havoc. I decided to immediately cut her off, and was actually quite puzzled at her behavior, as I truly had been conscientious of pacing our alcohol intake. That was my last complete thought before the blackness settled in. I only know the rest of the story after piecing together eyewitness accounts on the days following.

Carrie and I were somehow separated, and she was first found laying half on the sidewalk, half on the street, semi-conscious and mumbling about having to get away from the cops. Apparently some random guy passing by felt sorry for her and carried her to the parking garage, so she wasn't in plain view of passing police, which was obviously her prime concern. Unfortunately he wasn't the smartest man in the world, because (1) he laid her down in an actual parking space, and (2) he left her alone in a downtown parking garage late at night. She must have felt somewhat more secure, because she ended up passing out right where he left her until a lady found her some time later. Thank God for civic duty; this lady was a nurse and took over from there. Somehow Carrie was still in possession of her purse, and the woman used the available information and Carrie's cell phone to figure out who she was and whom to call, which unfortunately for Carrie and I ended up being her husband. Now, according to sources, when I was delivered unconscious to my apartment without Carrie, Dave knew well enough to know all was *not* well. He immediately called Mike to see if Carrie was home. Of course she wasn't, and panic ensued. Needless to say, by the time Mike received the call from the nurse, claiming to have retrieved his wife from a parking garage, he had been well-versed on my goings on and was uncharacteristically worried. The nurse ended up driving Carrie and her car home, while a friend followed behind in her car. What a sport that lady was. Carrie lived in a suburb of Wichita, so between getting her there and driving back, it was a good thirty miles out of that lady's way. Mike even tried to pay her when she safely delivered his wife and his car, and she wouldn't accept it. That's the chick you want to find you passed out in a public place!

As Carrie was sleeping on pavement, I was having my own adventure. I was found in the women's restroom, passed out in a stall, completely naked. Even though that sounds frightening, especially after knowing I was slipped a Mickey, I'm pretty sure I wasn't taken advantage of sexually. First of all, the women's restroom was always jam-packed in that place, with a long line leading down the hall. Second of all, I can see myself trying to go to the bathroom with the least amount of confinement, stripping myself of anything getting in my way and finally, exhausted from the effort, deciding to take a little nap on the grimy bathroom floor. That's how I roll. Thank God for small towns; one of my good friends, Jen, found me naked in the stall and took over from there. She enlisted the help of friends, and after dressing me carried me out through the back of the bar, before laying me on the cobblestone street, trying to decide what to do next. Because you can get arrested for public intoxication, they had to hurriedly lift me up and hold me *Weekend at Bernie's* style, when a cop drove slowly by, as they usually did every five minutes. He didn't stop, and when he was out of sight, they laid me back on the ground. Jen used her cell to get a hold of Dave to let him know what was going on. She told him she would take me home, but he had to meet us outside, because I was unconscious. My brother was lucky enough to have been hanging out with Dave, so they were both there to receive the limp body that was me. I didn't remain a corpse for long, because as soon as they tried to pull me out of the car, I started thrashing around, trying to fight my brother and my husband as they carried me toward our apartment (from corpse to flesh-eating zombie). Since they didn't carry as much empathy as Jen did, they grew tired of getting hit and just dropped me in the parking lot next to the curb (simultaneously, Carrie was, herself, laying in a parking lot). Apparently that knocked some sense into me (or out of me), as about ten minutes later I was unconscious again, and they were able to pick me back up and carry me inside, depositing me on the floor of our guest bathroom (see the theme?). I woke there at 5:30 a.m., totally confused and feeling sicker than I have ever felt in my whole life. As hard and cold as the floor was, I didn't want to move, but was soon forced to when I started dry-heaving and had to crawl to the toilet. I fell back asleep next to the toilet until Dave woke me up, telling me I had to get ready for breakfast. *Breakfast? Are you shitting me? Can't you see I'm having a near-death experience here?* I could tell Dave was completely disgusted as he reminded me that my dad and Bonus Mom were in town for Father's Day, and we were taking them out for breakfast. I had no choice but to put on my big girl panties and get up. Thank goodness I was already dressed and had makeup on (sort of) from the night before, because my body hurt so bad I couldn't even lay a finger on myself. Even my face hurt when I touched it to wipe the leftover vomit from the side of my mouth. As I was trying to make my hair look less like a troll doll, the nausea came back full-force. That was the start of my six-hour puke-fest.

We picked my parents up at their hotel, and they immediately asked what was wrong with me. At that point, I was still unable to comprehend what had happened, and hadn't heard any of the stories, so as far as everyone was concerned, I had just gotten dangerously wasted and acted completely irresponsibly. I felt like a total asshole. We went to The Good Egg, where I couldn't even look at anyone else's food, let alone eat some myself. I was in the bathroom every five minutes throwing up after seeing an egg yolk here, sausage patty there. Throughout breakfast, I could tell my Dad was pretty disappointed in me, so you can imagine how embarrassed I felt when we all had to trek to Heroes later that day to retrieve my debit card I had stupidly left behind. I was worried that my tab was going to be outrageous, as I had absolutely no recollection after the swing dancing moment, where I swear on my life, I had been totally sober. I was relieved to find that Heroes had my card, and my tab totaled a whopping $7.50. At least I had that going for me! It took us a couple of days of putting stories together before we figured out that we had been drugged. My brother's friends were at the bar at the same time, and saw us go from slightly tipsy to out of our minds in a matter of minutes. Because we were accepting drinks from total strangers, someone took the opportunity to slip something in one of them. At least they only enjoyed the after-effects from a distance, and didn't try to throw us in their trunks to rape us at the nearest playground! Carrie was totally traumatized by the whole thing. After my body stopped hurting a couple of days later, I was able to appreciate the humor and experience. I promised Carrie that one day she would think the whole thing was funny, which she had a hard time believing, but by now, of course, thinks it's hysterical…especially since some of the horrendous things that could have easily happened didn't. We didn't touch alcohol for months, which means we bumped up the marijuana intake. Doing so meant we had a lot more relaxing nights at home by the fire eating instead of out at the bars puking, which oddly enough ended up to be *more* adventurous, due to the crazy next-door neighbor that liked to stalk us.

Illegal drugs aren't the only things my body rejects mercilessly. Any chemical drug like allergy medicine, cold medicine, antibiotics, narcotics…forget it. The only thing I can take without an adverse reaction is Tylenol, and that's just because I can't see what it does to my liver. I get side-effects from drugs that are so uncommon, they aren't even listed as side-effects on the information sheets included in the box. I've heard "We need to take a picture of this for a medical journal" more times than I care to think about. Because of this, I use homeopathic remedies for almost everything, including my asthma. Instead of sucking on an inhaler and feeling like my heart is going to burst out of my chest from the rapid beating, I let a homeopathic asthma tablet melt under my tongue, with my lungs opening up not five minutes later and no side-effects, to boot. I use melatonin when I have problems sleeping, Arnica when I have sore muscles or bruising, and Apis for stings and bites. I will go full-force (that's full-force, not full-frontal, as that would only hurt my cause) against any idiot that claims homeopathy and holistic medicine is not effective. Ignorance breeds dumb fucks and those skeptics are one or the other. I'm living proof. I successfully use it for most anything that ails my family and pets. I recommend that every house get a homeopathic first-aid kit. Save your chemical and toxin intake for the things you can't control, like pollution or hair removal cream for your upper lip!

Unfortunately, my sensitivity to chemicals makes me a poor candidate for stimulants, which are primarily used to treat AD(H)D. It doesn't mean they don't work for me—they actually work too well. I become so intensely focused that it annoys the piss out of me when someone breaks my concentration. That doesn't make for a pleasant day with the kids (for them or me), as they are constantly talking and yipping and yapping, and I become incredibly impatient with the never-ending flow of interruptions (even if I'm just unloading the dishwasher). I've been off and on different medications and dosages hoping to find one that would give me the focus I need without the intensity it creates. It took three years, but I finally found one that almost works for me. Good old Ritalin. I say *almost* because I still can't take it when the kids are home. I've found that if I take it right after they leave for school, I'll get about four hours of good focus in before the medicine wears off in time for me to pick them up, fog-headed and scattered as usual. It's not ideal, but it makes for happier kids and a happier mama. I don't take the medicine every day, because I get a weird dermatitis if I take it consecutively (Medical Journal anyone?), and the only time I can't function without it is when I'm writing. It makes me wonder how I ever made it through school without medication. Because I don't have a completely healthy brain, I take brain supplements and regular supplements such as fish oil every day, which gives me better odds on those unmedicated days. I take 5-HTP for depression and Sam-e for the AD(H)D. Those two supplements work miracles for my mood and motivation.

If you're interested in treating your brain conditions naturally, I highly suggest you read Dr. Amen's book *Magnificent Mind at Any Age*. I consider that book my brain bible, and never have it farther than arm's distance away. There is even a supplement to treat men for "Grumpy Old Man Syndrome" or "manopause," which is due to the natural decline of serotonin as people age. Carrie has even been able to cure a lot of her control-freak tendencies just by taking a supplement. It's amazing to see her progress and even more amazing when she decides she feels great and doesn't need it anymore, and then slowly turns back into Mr. Hyde. I always tell her, "You feel great because you're taking it, dumbass; it's not because you've suddenly been cured!" She ignores me until she eventually recognizes she has gone back to the dark side, and starts taking them again. I don't want to sound like I am a perfect vitamin-taker. I usually forget on the weekends, because there's less structure. It only takes a couple of days for me to figure out that I haven't taken them, because the first sign is my ability to cry at anything. If after that I don't start back on them immediately, I'll soon graduate into a funk. I try not to let myself get that far, because the funk takes about five or six days to dissipate even after I get those supplements in my system. However, shit happens and if I end up there, I just tell myself over and over that *I don't really feel this way. My brain just thinks I do, but I don't. These are not really my emotions. My brain is just seeing things wonky. This is not me.* It sounds like a bad case of denial, but it really helps by allowing me to detach myself from the pressure of owning that depressed state. It's not me, dammit—it's my goofy brain! I may be affected by these hopeless feelings, but they're not mine, so there's no reason to be consumed by them. Instead I push through the emotions and the minutes, never seeing the light at the end until I suddenly stumble into it and once again feel glad to have made it through in one piece. I think not ever seeing that light coming up is what makes depressed people think they'll never feel better than they do at that moment. Reminding myself that the light has never failed me allows me to go with the flow of my mood instead of fighting it, which makes the trip a lot more bearable.

Chapter 23

You say *tomato*, I say *fuck you*.

I've always been a procrastinator. I'm talking, my entire life. As a kid, my procrastinating tendencies were all but impossible to control. It was the way I was, and I had no idea there was anything wrong with it. As I grew up, I became aware that procrastinating wasn't a very mature thing to do, and spent massive amounts of energy trying to be more responsible. As I had my own kids, I no longer had the extra oomph it took for me to fight my ways, and I once again became irresponsible and a procrastinator. I make it sound like it was an easy transition, but it wasn't. When I finally realized I couldn't keep all of those balls in the air, I spent a good amount of time in the dead place. I absolutely despised myself for being such a complete and utter fucking loser. I even tried to share my thoughts in a journal, but only succeeded in splattering the page with venom and rage. I still have the journal, and when I read it now, it gives me a good case of the giggles. I can't believe I was so angry! Here's the actual first passage for you; I was still two long years away from being diagnosed, but had always joked that I had AD(H)D.

August 7th, 2004

I have to start this journal by stating that there are so many things about myself that I hate, it will be many journals before I'm finished naming them. As soon as I lifted this journal off the shelf, I got the same feeling in the pit of my stomach that I always do…greasy disgust and the rotten stench of failure. I'll never write in here. Who am I kidding? It's the story of my life. I'm a loser. I still feel lucky to have my family and friends, so why isn't that enough? What the fuck is my problem? I guess that's what I'm searching for. The answer to the million-dollar question. Forgive me ahead of time for my language. I don't use it because I'm bitter or from the wrong side of the tracks. I honestly just think it's funny and adds flair to stories…then you basically just get into a habit. Before you know it, you've used the "f" word eight times just to give someone directions to the nearest gas station. Anyway…back to my story…oh, don't mind the ADD either…along with, oh yeah, I hate the term ADHD. It's just like I hate when people say DWI instead if DUI. When people pronounce the "w," they always say "dub-ya." D dub-ya I. It really pisses me off. Or when a business intentionally misspells a word. There's a gas station down the street called "Kum-n-go"—that annoys the crap out of me.

I feel sorry for that girl up there! I really, truly thought I was a despicable person just because I….*murdered someone?* No. *Killed small animals for sport?*… No. *Robbed an elderly lady?* No. I have AD(H)D, and that requires me to procrastinate—the sin of all sins, as some would like you to think! But guess what? I'm actually not a loser. Without the executive function skills normal people have, procrastination is the only way my brain knows to get me to complete tasks, but hey, at least it thought of something! It takes the pressure of that deadline to light up that task-completing part of my brain, but it ends with the same results as someone that hasn't procrastinated. I can honestly say that in my adult life I've never missed a deadline. So, my question is, who says which way is better? You say *tomato,* I say *fuck you.* That never gets old. My other favorite saying is, "Does my fat ass make my ass look fat?" Anyway, back to my original point, though I mostly use it for motivation, procrastination isn't always the result of attempting to get motivated. It can also be caused by dead brain. Dead brain sucks. Sometimes, especially if I'm overwhelmed, my poor brain just comes to a complete halt and ceases to work. Since I have the annoying ability to become overwhelmed by any common, everyday duties, as you can imagine, something as basic as e-mail is my personal hell. It's a constant struggle for me. The more e-mail that comes in, the more I withdraw from checking it, the more it builds up, and it just progresses to this monster that terrorizes me daily with guilt, shame, and anxiety, because I'm not on top of it. As painful as those feelings are, I am still simply unable to force myself to check my e-mail. Unbelievable. I know, it looks like procrastination, but really, my brain is stuck, and it's not budging until it gets some things figured out. I don't know how to help the poor thing when it's like that, so I go to outside help, namely Dave and my mom. Here's a recent text between my husband and I. This is an actual text, and what prompted me to touch on the subject. Oh yeah...if you don't get my husband's sense of humor, it's OK; sometimes I don't either. The point is, sometimes I just have to ask for help, and I don't feel bad about it one bit.

Stacey: You're going to have to force me to answer my e-mail tonight. Use physical force if necessary; I'm simply not capable.

Dave: I will use the force, Yoda.

Stacey: Thankful, I am.

Dave: LOL, I am.

Stacey: You just went too far.

Dave: Legend, I am.

Stacey: Not at all funny.

I often have to call my mom to help me prioritize a nonexistent to-do list that I'd been too overwhelmed to even create. My mental to-do list items do not naturally fall into place of importance as I'm tossing them around violently in my head. Imagine my mind as a snow globe and my thoughts as the glitter. Now turn it upside down and shake it like you mean it. That's great, but for good measure, set it on the ground. Take ten steps back. Now take off and run as fast as you can, kicking the shit out of the snow globe when you reach it. Now, run after it, pick it up, shake the crap out of it again, and then watch the glitter. See what I mean? Beautiful chaos. It's cool to look at, but when it's the contents of your mind, you can't make heads or tails out of that stuff floating around in there. That's when I start to freak out and call my mom. At that point, she has to grab on to some of those shiny, little floaters and expertly extract any important items or issues from my big, snow-globe head. When she's confident she's made all necessary extractions, she breaks my thoughts down into "smaller, more manageable pieces," as she likes to say. It's not until she breaks it all down that I'm mentally able to participate in the prioritization process. Otherwise, it's all just a big blob of stuff bouncing around in my brain, confusing the hell out me.

I think I'm missing some kind of processing chip, too, now that I think about it. It's probably the same reason I'm unable to process a long conversation in real time. It's not until later, maybe hours, that I'll replay the entire conversation for myself, sometimes multiple times, before I'm able to process the entirety of what was said. It wasn't until McLovin brought that act to my attention that I thought anything of it.

McLovin: Do you always go over every detail of every conversation you've ever had after it's already happened?

Me: (with food in my mouth) Yeah.

McLovin: Do you think that's normal?

Me: (surprised, and still with food in my mouth) Yeah?

McLovin: No.

Me: Huh.

That "weirdo revelation" in a conversation is never fun, because for the most part, I recognize my differences and accept them, but it's never fun finding out that I'm doing something weird that I had no clue was considered weird! It's really unsettling, and I start to worry about my judgment. Now that I think about it, that little brain fart of a thought up there should probably the actual definition of *weirdo* in the dictionary!

Weirdo: weird o, (wîr dō), n pl -dos, -dies – One who does things considered weird, without realizing said things are considered weird.

So…mystery solved. It's not the other people, as I've always expected…I *am* actually *weird. Huh.*

I think I've made a pretty good case for why it's incredibly important (sometimes literally life-or-death) for people like myself to have at least one personal cheerleader that will love us unconditionally, and never judge, try to fix us, or make us feel shameful about how we were wired. Changing the perception of my actions for those around me was a huge undertaking. It was important to me that they understood how my brain worked in order for them to truly understand how I ticked. I passed around every article or book passage I came across that would hopefully explain away every quality I was pretty sure people hated about me. Educate. Educate. Educate. My poor friends and family. Their inherited "AD(H)D/Giftedness" coach positions are not for the weak of heart, but they always rally for me. I know they love me, and are happy to make deposits in my mental health bank by working me through my quirks. I finally realized that all of that silly stuff like organization, time management, and pre-planning is overrated and has absolutely no bearing on my intelligence. I'm still smart as a whip. Well…I am when I'm not busy being a dumbass.

After my diagnosis, I did a lot of research online. I'll never forget stumbling across the previous mentioned article, by Thom Hartmann. It completely changed my warped perception of myself, and I think of it often.

I was in India in 1993 to help manage a community for orphans and blind children on behalf of a German charity. During the monsoon season, the week of the big Hyderabad earthquake, I took an all-day train ride almost all the way across the subcontinent (from Bombay through Hyderabad to Rajamundri) to visit an obscure town near the Bay of Bengal. In the train compartment with me were several Indian businessmen and a physician, and we had plenty of time to talk as the countryside flew by from sunrise to sunset.

Curious about how they viewed our children diagnosed as having Attention Deficit Hyperactivity Disorder (ADHD), I asked, "Are you familiar with those types of people who seem to crave stimulation, yet have a hard time staying with any one focus for a period of time? They may hop from career to career and sometimes even from relationship to relationship, never seeming to settle into one job or into a life with one person—but the whole time they remain incredibly creative and inventive."

"Ah, we know this type well," one of the men said, the other three nodding in agreement.

"What do you call this personality type?" I asked.

"Very holy," he said. "These are old souls, near the end of their karmic cycle."

Again, the other three nodded agreement, perhaps a bit more vigorously in response to my startled look.

"Old souls?" I questioned, thinking that a very odd description for those whom American psychiatrists have diagnosed as having a particular disorder.

"Yes," the physician said. "In our religion, we believe that the purpose of reincarnation is to eventually free oneself from worldly entanglement and desire. In each lifetime we experience certain lessons, until finally we are free of this earth and can merge into the oneness of God. When a soul is very close to the end of those thousands of incarnations, he must take a few lifetimes to do many, many things—to clean up the little threads left over from his previous lives."

"This is a man very close to becoming enlightened," a businessman added. "We have great respect for such individuals, although their lives may be difficult."

Another businessman raised a finger and interjected. "But it is through the difficulties of such lives that the soul is purified."

The others nodded agreement.

"In America they consider this behavior indicative of a psychiatric disorder," I said.

All three looked startled, then laughed.

"In America you consider our most holy men, our yogis and swamis, to be crazy people as well," said the physician with a touch of sadness in his voice. "So it is with different cultures. We live in different worlds."

We in our Western world have such "holy" and nearly enlightened people among us and we say they must be mad. But as we're about to see, they may instead be our most creative individuals, our most extraordinary thinkers, our most brilliant inventors and pioneers. The children among us whom our teachers and psychiatrists say are "disordered" may, in fact, carry a set of abilities—a skill set—that was necessary for the survival of humanity in the past, that has created much of what we treasure in our present "quality of life," and that will be critical to the survival of the human race in the future.[1]

Isn't that a cool story? We're old souls! I'm embarrassed to tell you that I tried levitating after I read it, and I'm sorry to report I wasn't able to. My stomach was growling, and that was really distracting, but some day I may try levitating again. Needless to say, sometimes I forget to focus on my gifts, and sometimes I forget I even have any, but we all need to hear it, and I was reminded of that when I was in California last summer for my friend's wedding. I got to talking to my other friend, who owns a medicinal marijuana shop. I knew that he had AD(H)D, so we compared notes and found that his brain worked almost identical to mine! The difference is that I've totally

---

1   Thom Hartmann, excerpt from introduction to *The Edison Gene: ADHD and the Gift of the Hunter Child* (Rochester, VT: Park Street Press, 2003). Excerpt available at http://www.thomhartmann.com/blog/2003/01/edison-gene-adhd-gifted-creative.

accepted, and can now even appreciate, that I'll never have perfect mental health and he's still in the horrendous self-loathing stage. We went out back during the reception and smoked a joint (business expense?) as he poured his heart out about all of the things that he felt were "wrong" about him. Since I'd already been down that road, I thought I'd save him some pavement pounding, and give him a shortcut to self-acceptance by giving him my philosophy and some short stories to accompany it. Due to time constraints, I was obviously not able to tell him every thought I had on the subject, but when he suddenly felt accepted and understood, his tears began falling, and that moment had a profound effect on me. I truly understood why it was so important for me to finish writing the monstrous manuscript of which the cerebral weight felt like a grown man riding around on my head all hours of the day. There was finally a tangible purpose for me to focus on, and at that moment, I was instantly convinced that I did actually have something meaningful to say, and even though I curse a bit, there are jewels of wisdom amidst the colorful language. I want to give something special to all of the extraordinary and misunderstood people out there, just like me...acceptance and high fives. That's right—acceptance of myself and others and good old high fives. If every human practiced those things on a daily basis, there would be collectively more peace and happiness in all of our lives. I believe the world can be a better place; I truly do. But until everyone is allowed to be, and most importantly, celebrated for being the people they were destined to be, the doors leading to some of our most important riches and discoveries will remain tightly locked, and gifts that should have and definitely would have been presented to the world, and widely celebrated by all, will remain behind those locked doors in a dusty box, hidden by shadows, untouched and unopened, as if they never even existed. Meanwhile, the soul, aware of its own magic, will move through life from birth to death, with every fiber of its being silently screaming that all is not as it should be. It's heartbreaking, and I simply can't stand the thought of what humanity has already lost to those dusty boxes. That's why it's time to get our freak on, people. *Here's to not catching our hair on fire!*

Epilogue

*I*t's been nearly two years since I started this book. As you can imagine, there have been some changes in the meantime. I'm no longer on the board of the PTA. I just couldn't do it anymore; that yearbook sucked the life out of me! Now I'm just a minion in the environmental group. It doesn't take a lot of time, but I feel like I'm accomplishing more positive things for the school. I'm also just a regular volunteer instead of the room mom. Dave got a new job, so he ditched the rust bucket when he acquired a company car. We lost Yin Yang a couple of months ago to cancer, and though I talk to his little cedar box often, I've really missed having him around as my silent, yet stinky, partner.

I have to say that writing the manuscript was, by far, the most challenging thing I have put myself through to date. Notice, I said *to date*. Who knows what kooky thing I'll come up with next! I am wondering, though, who thought it was a good idea for ADD girl to try to focus on something that requires more focus than most anything else? Writing a book? Am I nuts? What happened to baby steps? I guess sometimes giant steps are needed. Giant steps aren't nearly as comfortable, but you cover a lot more ground in a shorter amount of time. It's been frustrating, challenging, and sometimes even physically painful to pull my thoughts together in a somewhat sensical manner for you. Is *sensical* even a word? If not, it should be. There's no word that makes more sense there than sensical! Anyway, as I begin the end, I'm rifling through the nonalphabetized files in my brain, making sure I covered every freak flag I want to fly. Of course, I haven't flown them all, as some belong in that elusive "other book." Isn't it crazy that I'm so weird that it takes two books to talk about why and how? Who is *that* weird? Actually, I think you'd be surprised. But you know what's even crazier? I absolutely love myself for the same reason. Two books-worth of nonconformity is quite an honor! It just took me a while to realize it. Experiencing the transition from self-loathing to self-acceptance has been an intense, painful, enlightening, frightening, exciting, ball-busting journey, and now I can honestly say there is absolutely nothing I would change about myself. Sure I still get pissed at myself and my brain, but now my love is unconditional. I taught myself and those around me to focus on my gifts and to laugh with me at the silliness of my "deficits" because in my world, they aren't deficits: they're actually the norm, and those other guys are the weirdoes! Hey, I'm not making this stuff up; maybe you're just dimensionally challenged.

Texas, January 2011

Acknowledgments

I'd like to start off by thanking my wacky brain for giving all of its might to get through the whole gnarly book process from pen to press. I know it wasn't easy, but you chugged along and hung in there until the very end, like a pro. Well done, my friend. Well done.

I can't gush enough about the sacrifices my husband, Dave has made to get this book out of my head and into your hands. He spent a good portion of the last couple of years working during the day and then in the evenings while I wrote; herding the kids, burning dinner, screwing up laundry, and then dropping them off with the grandparents when his sanity began to slide. I'm that lucky. I just hope he knows how much I love him and appreciate the effort, no matter the outcome of my favorite white t-shirt.

Special Thanks To:

The kids for tipping me over the edge to this side of crazy. Without you, I wouldn't have known how nuts I could get and still make it back to sanity in one piece. Thank you for teaching me the art of patience and making me love something fiercely enough to fight for it.

My mom and dad for gently pushing me in my own direction, never demanding to know my destination or what road I was taking to get there. You've taught me that it's truly the journey that matters most.

My brother for always being the Clyde to my Bonnie no matter where we lived. There's something reassuring in the fact that there's always someone standing by, waiting to beat up pimply Kindergarteners named Nathaniel, that won't leave me alone.

My bonus-parents for putting up with a bunch of crap from a kid that isn't even yours, and for always making me feel like I *am*.

My brothers and sisters-in-law for letting my favorite nieces and nephew hang out with their crazy Aunt Safety that loves cats and dogs, and teaches them animal reflexology when they come to visit.

My in-laws for having Dave and the kids over for dinner many a night while I wrote this book, and for sending the "good salad" home so I could eat as well.

My animals; Stormi T., Ernie Girl, Owen Bella, Rock Star Xavier, and Yin Yang (RIP), for always offering a warm, soft place to lay my hands when I was procrastinating. It allowed me to take breaks I never felt guilty for.

My family and friends far and wide for loving me wholly and organically. There's no better gift in the world...

Dr. Ned Hallowell, whom I've never met but has saved my life and deeply impacted my perception of who I am and what I have to offer the world in the best way possible.

Sarah Cypher at *The Threepenny Editor* (www.threepennyeditor.com) for giving me direction when I stood at a double fork in the bumpy road of publishing. If it weren't for you, I'd still be there, walking in circles and mumbling to myself about query letters.

Dena Graziano, because she insisted that I add her name here.

Author Biography

Stacey Turis is an adult living with ADHD and giftedness who earned her degree in broadcast journalism from Wichita State University. She co-produced and hosted a TV show for a FOX affiliate before pursuing a career in advertising, then graphic design, then market research, then photography, then IT, then acting, then...

In 2006, she became certified to teach Yoga but didn't, then founded pawsforpeace.com, an online, holistic pet-health site, with an iPhone app called Dr. Shawn's Natural Pet Therapies to match. In 2010, she developed a course to teach families how to live more natural lifestyles, which she taught for about a month. She then started a Facebook page called ADHD - Tales of an Absent-Minded Superhero, for wacky folks like herself. *That* is still exciting enough to hold her interest. She has, through the years, unsuccessfully started twenty-seven businesses but can't remember most of them. She lives in Texas with her husband, two kids, a dog, three cats, and eight goldfish. Stacey now spends her time speaking to groups of those same kinds of wacky people, where she's not afraid to stop in the middle of a speech and ask "What was I talking about?" You can learn more at www.staceyturis.com.